The HOUSEKEEPER'S *Secret*

A WHIRLIGIG CHRISTMAS

CAROL FRENCH-COBB

The Housekeeper's Secret
A Whirligig Christmas

Print ISBN: 978-1-66783-8-021

eBook ISBN: 978-1-66783-8-038

THANKS

Writing the love story of Emma and Michael was a pleasure no matter how long it took me to finished. My first draft readers were so supportive and gave me great feedback. Laura Hill held a zoom conference with me and gave excellent suggestions for the story line, Jenn Krpan loved the chapter names and thought they were funny, Jane Brueggemann had helpful thoughts as to the characters, and Pat Hurst loved the story line and said not to change it. Editors are different with their sharp eye to particular words, spelling, syntax, and the need to be very honest, which I appreciated. Gail Haack, my first editor, kept me on track chapter by chapter, and Amy Cobb, a school librarian, put a youthful spin on some of the characters. And I give a shout out to my computer-editing buddy, Grammarly, which was helpful with phrasing and word choice. All that said, any mistakes are all my own.

DEDICATION

I dedicate this book to the people who face danger in foreign lands and people who face danger here in America. This is a love letter to the people of the Midwest who show compassion and kindness to strangers. To Paul Fleischman who gave me permission to mention his wonderful young adult novel, Whirligig, in my book as well as excellent advice to make the story my own.

chapter one

...in which their travels come to an end at
The Coffee Bean and Chicken Café

The snowflakes were falling as Emma walked down the hill from the train station. Dusk was early this time of year. She pulled her hair back into a low ponytail, which slipped throughout the two days traveling. She stood up straight, although her backpack was digging into her side. The baby carrier also seemed to get heavier with each step.

She stopped and switched arms. The baby didn't seem as heavy as the backpack, but she smiled every time the girl looked at her sweet face. Nothing seemed to bother her. A few months over a year old, she was thoroughly charming and happy. Her real name was Charlotte, but she was called Charlie almost immediately after birth. It just seemed to fit.

Emma readjusted her coat closer around her neck and pulled up the hood. "It's getting colder, Charlie. I don't want you to get a cold. Thanksgiving is just around the corner, and no one wants to be sick around the holidays." She talked to Charlie as if the baby understood everything she was saying.

She continued down the hill noticing all the houses on either side of the street. From this viewpoint, the little town was picturesque with tidy lawns and well-kept streets. She passed a colorful welcome sign for the village with a whirligig beside it with a Christmas scene. The whirligigs' blades moved Santa up and down as he put presents under a Christmas tree. The sign promoted the town Christmas Festival coming up the week before Christmas.

There was a glow coming from the windows of the houses. Emma felt a little lonely on the sidewalk looking into homes with families, but somehow Emma felt optimistic. Maybe this would be the right place to settle down. Heaven knows how to find a job, but she thought she could do reception or waitress work. She had taken quite a few classes in college. She felt almost cheerful as she reached the bottom of the hill.

The station manager had told her that the town's center was at the bottom of the first hill. As she looked down, she noticed what looked like a city hall in a square. There were harvest decorations in front of the building with giant pumpkins, gourds, and hay bales. Twinkling lights decorated the building next to the City Hall. It must be a café of some sort, the girl thought. The connecting streets all seemed to be hilly and curvy. The name of the town, Hill Brook, seemed to fit. The girl had seen a sign, 'Best little town west of the Mississippi River,' when she left the train station. It was a cute name for a small town—just as good a place as any to settle. She wondered where the brook was if there was one.

"I need a coffee, and Charlie needs a diaper change, food, and milk," she said to no one. I am starting to talk to myself." Before she pushed open the front door of the café with its green shutters and colorful awning, she looked up and down the main street. They were the same style, with red accents over the fronts of the buildings. It looked as if these shop owners planned to look so charming. All the lampposts were black and had old-fashioned lamps at the top that appeared to be gas but were solar-powered. That was impressive in a small town. She opened the door of the café after reading the sign over the door. Inside she immediately felt the warmth, both natural and in feeling. The name of the restaurant made her smile. The Coffee Bean and Chicken Café had a counter toward the side and tables and chairs with red-checkered tablecloths. She remembered the train master said children named the café, which was certainly unique.

The waitress behind the counter holding the menus said cheerily, "Come on in and have a seat anywhere. I'll be right with you."

The girl wondered if this was Nelly that the station volunteer, Harry, had mentioned, but she seemed too young. Charlie was squirming in her car seat, anxious to get out. She was just about to start crawling on her own, and she loved to try it out and even tried to pull herself up on chairs. Walking was right around the corner. Babies seem to change every day!

"Come on, Charlie, let's get you out of there. It has been a long day," Emma said to the squirming child. The waitress handed her a menu and brought a high chair that looked like it had been here for several generations of customers.

"Do you have a place I could change the baby?"

"Sure do. I've got a nice changing table a family donated after their last child grew out of diapers. Real nice back there if I do say so myself." She pointed to a door in the back of the café.

"Thanks." Emma grabbed the backpack and carried Charlie toward the restroom. She looked around the dining room and noticed several couples eating dinner. Emma saw a few customers eating chicken in one type of dish or another. Two police officers by the windows turned to look at her walking through the restaurant. As she went into the restroom, she noticed a man slumped in a chair by the windows with his legs propped up on another chair. His worn cowboy hat was down over his face, so she couldn't tell how old he was. She quietly passed him, not wanting to speak with anyone. She didn't like the police officers to notice her at all.

The restroom was nice and cozy, and the changing table was very homelike. The girl looked around and wistfully thought of home and all she had left behind. Then, shaking her head, she felt it was worth it. It was time to move on.

She washed her hands and splashed water all over her face. It felt good, but what she would love was a hot bath or shower.

Coming back into the dining room, she noticed the man hadn't moved, and no one seemed to be paying any attention to him. The customers sat throughout the restaurant, but there was a comfortable level of quiet conversation at each table. It was a nice feeling to be among them, even though she didn't know anyone here. The police officers stood and paid their bill, leaving without talking to anyone. Finally, the shorter man turned and looked back at her. She turned her head toward Charlie impulsively. It was hard not to look as if something was wrong.

The waitress came back and waited while the girl put Charlie into the highchair.

"Can I get you something to drink?" she asked.

"I would love hot coffee, and could I have some milk for the baby?"

"Sure. What's the little gal's name?"

"Her name is Charlotte, but we call her Charlie."

"Cute. I will be right back with your drinks." The girl watched as the waitress went back to the kitchen. She had comfortable shoes, and she tied her hair into a ponytail. Maybe Nelly was in the kitchen. It seems, sometimes, that all the people in a small town knew each other in some way.

The simple menu offered tasty, hearty meals for a chilly evening. The girl decided to have the chicken and dumplings, which Charlie could share. The meal sounded so good to her after the half sandwich on the train. Something warm would help, too. She chuckled to herself about the name of the Chicken Café.

The hot coffee was delicious, and Charlie enjoyed her milk as they waited, and Emma looked out the front window at the little town. She just needed some time to get her bearings. Her grandma used to say that to her when Emma was deciding something. Maybe she could get a job and find someone to watch Charlie part of the time. Her money supply would run out before too long.

The waitress came over with her plate of chicken and dumplings. It was steamy, just the way it should be.

"You're new in town?" The waitress asked in a friendly manner.

"I am. The station manager mentioned he knew the owner, Nelly. Is she here?"

"She is busy in the kitchen. She might have time to come and talk to you. Could I help you? My name is Jennifer Coggan. I just started working here because I am saving money for college. I hope to start after high school if I earn enough money."

"Congratulations, and good luck. It is nice to meet you. I will try to stop in and talk to Nelly later. Do you know a place I could stay tonight or maybe a little longer?"

"The boarding house up the street might have a room left. It is a slow time of year. The owner likes to call it a Bed and Breakfast, but people tend to stay like an old-fashioned boarding house for a long while. The town will get bustling as we get closer to Christmas. We will pick up business once the holiday visitors come to town."

"Why do people come here for Christmas?" the girl asked.

"All the businesses participate in the festival, and a church in town has a wonderful Christmas pageant every year. People come from all around to see it. My grandmother has lived here all her life. Just about everyone in the town has some part in it. The ladies make all kinds of Christmas decorations and crafts of all types to sell for our Holiday Festival. The hardware store in Hill Brook sells seasonal whirligigs and garden elves. They always have customers come from all over to purchase them." The waitress took a breath and added, "This is a nice place to be during December. This area hasn't had snow the past few years, but maybe we will this year. It makes everything so much more festive." She stopped talking, realizing she kept the girl from eating the hot meal. "I will bring you more coffee and let you eat in peace."

Emma cut up small pieces for Charlie, who was jiggling in her chair, anxious for a taste. They both enjoyed the warmth of the meal and the dish's flavor. She enjoyed the last few bites when she saw the sleepy man was paying his bill and leaving the café. He was facing the cash register, so she couldn't look at him without turning around in her chair. She was curious about the man but didn't want to attract notice. Charlie started to bounce up and down about that time, waving her chubby arms in the air. Finally, the man stomped out, and the door slammed behind him.

The waitress was back and just rolled her eyes, not saying anything about the rude man. She slipped the bill under the plate and said, "Pay me whenever you are ready to go."

"Thanks, the chicken and dumplings were wonderful, especially on a cold, dreary day."

"Nelly always tries to make them on days like this." The waitress winked and said, "We do a lot of chicken dishes. Thanks for coming in today. If you are still interested in the boarding house, it is just a block and a half to the right when you come out of the café. It is called the Hibiscus Home Bed and Breakfast. Millie, the owner, makes breakfast which she includes in the cost of the night."

"Thanks for the help," the girl said as she put on her coat and then helped Charlie into hers.

As she opened the door, a light mist was falling, and she hurried as best she could with the baby in the car seat and her backpack. The Hibiscus Home Bed and Breakfast sign was just up the hill on the next block. The train station manager wasn't kidding when he said there were hills. This hill was the opposite of coming into town. Since there was a light on the porch, the girl hoped that the owner had a room for her. The front porch was a wrap-around and had an incredible wooden swing at the corner. Her dad had always wanted one, but their porch didn't have enough room. She wondered about the name of the place.

She knocked lightly on the red front door because she couldn't find a doorbell. Different colored pumpkins decorated the porch with a colorful scarecrow creating a homey feeling. Then, just a moment later, she saw movement through the beveled glass window on the door. The woman was wiping her hands on a towel as she hurried to the door. "Hello, there, come on in out of the mist. It just might turn into snow this year. We can hope."

The girl stepped inside, setting her backpack and the baby carrier on the floor. "I was hoping you had a room for us tonight. We just arrived in town."

"I do have an available room on the third floor. My other guests have preferred the ground floor and second floor. No one has a little bit of adventure in their soul, if I do say so. The room is a little turret on the west side with the cutest windows in front. You will like the room, I know. By the way, my name is Millie Wilson."

The girl felt comfortable right away with the owner. Her pretty hair was rolled up neatly in the back, reminding the girl of her grandmother's hair. The owner had a calico apron over a neatly ironed dress. A fire in the fireplace and light jazz playing on the sound system was warm and cozy after her long travels.

"Nice to meet you. How much is the room?" the girl asked nervously, worried that the amount would be too much for her meager budget. So she didn't mention her name.

"It is sixty-five dollars, including breakfast. I also have a portable crib you can use. I will have my helper take it up in a little bit. Is that okay?"

Emma nodded and then sighed, realizing that her money would not last very long at this rate, but she had no choice. Her decision to leave her home was quick, but there was no going back. "That will be fine," she responded.

"Let me take your backpack, and you take the baby. We can climb those stairs in a jiffy." The girl had no idea how old the woman was, even with her silver hair. She sure could climb stairs well, no matter her age.

The girl climbed behind the lady, realizing she hadn't signed a register or shared her name with the owner. The few town people she met so far were so pleasant. She had heard that the Midwest was a friendly place, but she grew up farther east; this was shocking.

"When you get the baby settled for the night, come back down for a cup of tea, and we can fill out the registration card."

Tea sounded so warming, and Charlie was already getting sleepy, which a visit might be okay. The woman opened the door with a large old-fashioned key and showed the girl a small room with a turret. The curved windows surrounded the bedroom with starched frilly Pricilla curtains. The patchwork quilt and a pretty blue dust ruffle looked so comfortable.

"We do share bathrooms on each level, but yours is right next door. You can tell if someone is in there by the small Do Not Disturb sign hanging on the doorknob. Simple, but it works. Now, you get settled, and I will have my helper bring up the portable crib. Nice to have you here."

The girl felt like crying, but she smiled at Millie, saying, "Thanks so much."

The door closed quietly. The girl looked slowly around the room with its charming antiques and cozy feel. The bed felt comfortable as she picked up Charlie, hugging her and kissing her neck. "We made it, Charlie!" She felt safer than she had felt in days.

After changing her diaper and giving the baby the rest of the restaurant's milk, she played with her while waiting for the portable crib. Millie's teenage helper entered the bedroom moments later.

It was nice to have them arrange for a small crib. "Thanks so much. What's your name?"

"Julie Jordan. I just work here part-time while still in high school," she said as she started to leave the room. "Oh, what a cute baby," she said, tickling her under her chin.

Julie watched as the girl put Charlie down in the crib. She snuggled down quickly, and her eyes slowly closed. "Have a good night," she said as she left the room. The girl smiled back at her as Julie closed the door. The girl realized the teenager had not asked her her name either.

Emma wondered about what it was like to be a teenager in a small town. Looking over at Charlie in the little crib, a peaceful feeling washed over her. People in a small town are so friendly and helpful. Charlie was sleeping quietly, unaware of the turmoil in her young life. As Emma lay on her back, waiting for Charlie to fall asleep, she noticed that the ceiling was a beautiful tin embossed design.

Not sure of what the next day would bring, the girl was reviewing in her mind the money she had with her. She had closed her checking account and had not used any credit cards on the trip. She thought she had enough money to last a few weeks without finding a job. Her dad had given her as much cash as she felt comfortable carrying around. After that, she would have to get a job. The worst part was that she could not contact anyone who helped her getaway.

First thing tomorrow, she planned on looking through the local newspaper and hoped to locate some work she could do with a child in tow. One side of the room had a little turret, but the house's front side had a roof stuck out from home. The gable window reminded her of something she used to do as a teenager. She would put a pillow on the gable window's windowsill in the upstairs of her home and sit and look out at the stars and wonder about her future. She always asked if she would find a man as unique as her dad on those nights. Clouds covered the stars, but the memory was a sweet one.

Her thoughts brought back memories of her long journey to Hill Brook, remembering where she was. Finally, she realized leaving was the only answer to their problems. The past two days were scary, but it was exciting at the same time. She would never forget the people along the way who helped her getaway, including her family.

cнapter two

…in which the girl remembers their travels
beginning on a snowy night

As tiny as light raindrops, snow flurries started to drift steadily as Emma and Charlie left the car's warmth. Her tears were falling onto her turtleneck because she didn't have a spare hand to wipe them away. The car door slammed as she hurried away so that no one would notice her. She couldn't afford a backward glance, as she wasn't sure if someone was watching for her. The car drove away. The bus station was less crowded this time of night, but the waiting room's darkness and chill gave her an ominous feeling. She usually wasn't paranoid, but now she was.

"Two tickets to St. Louis, please," she said to the ticket master. He looked as if he were almost asleep.

"That will be $150, Miss. But, of course, the baby is free if she sits on your lap."

"Thank you," she answered. She hoped there would be an empty seat on the bus this late at night. A glance at the clock over the ticket window indicated almost midnight. The baby was sound asleep and unaware of the girl's stress.

Emma sat down on the bench and realized it looked as if the seats were pews from an old church. The baby kept sleeping, and all she could hope was that the child would sleep through the night. Emma loosened the baby's coat so Charlie wouldn't get overly warm. She didn't take off her jacket, as she didn't want to attract any more attention than necessary. Her mind started wandering, and Emma thought about the challenging year since the baby was born. She kept her face down if anyone came into the station that might recognize her. The bus had just pulled up, and several travelers got off, but luckily, they did not come into the station.

A few minutes later, the bus driver got off, and another driver came up and shook the ticket master's hand. "Time to board, Miss," he said.

She hoped this bus wouldn't be crowded. When she climbed up the steps, she was relieved to see just a few passengers scattered around the bus. Several people appeared to be asleep, which was good. She found a window seat, and the baby carrier fits right in the place next to her. She fastened the seat belt about the carrier's front if the bus came to an abrupt stop.

She felt relatively comfortable as the bus rolled out of the station heading west to St. Louis. The ticket was reasonable enough, but she wasn't sure her money would hold out until she found a safe place. She was pretty sure that no one was around the bus station when her dad had dropped her off. The baby kept sleeping, unaware of the turmoil around her. The girl took off her coat and leaned the seat back to rest a little herself or close her eyes. She gently placed a hand on the baby's arm. It was going to be a long night and day ahead.

She dozed off and on for about an hour or so until the baby started to fuss a little. Luckily the girl had a dry mix and water to prepare a bottle. She hoped the milk would keep the baby full until morning to feed her some cereal and baby fruit. She picked her up and cuddled her close, and luckily that was all it took. She fell back asleep.

The next thing she knew, a woman across from her woke her up and said, "We are taking a little break before continuing to St. Louis. Would you like a chance to feed and change your baby?"

"Thank you, that does sound good to stretch my legs and change her diaper. It is hard to change a baby on a bus," the girl said, smiling shyly at the woman.

While she was sleeping, she learned that the bus had been stopped at a station some miles back but was making good time coming into Illinois. It didn't matter to the girl as long as she got far away. The rest stop was almost empty in the morning, so a visit to the restroom went well, and the girl stopped to buy a donut for herself and get milk for the baby. She was careful not to have eye contact with many people. She laughed silently to herself, feeling like she had just broken out of prison. It was funny, but she was trying to lighten up the tension in her neck.

They boarded the bus quickly and continued the trip west. She had no idea where she would end up. The woman who woke her before asked, "Where are you headed?"

"Well, I'm transferring at Kirkwood's train station to go to Kansas City on the train." She made that up on the spot. "Not sure how I will do that, but I will figure it out." When Emma was in college in Missouri, she had a friend from the St. Louis suburb and thought it could be a place to stay.

"You are in luck. I left my car at the bus station, and I live in Kirkwood, so I can drop you off."

After the woman's kind offer of a ride to the train station, they talked for the next couple of hours. Although she made up her first name just for this moment, they shared names, so she said, Dottie. She had no idea how she thought of that name. The woman just announced her name was Jane, and she had just visited her cousin in Manhattan. Emma didn't want to mention that she had lived across the Hudson River from New York City. She cautiously told her name, hoping she wouldn't be telling too many lies. (Are lies wrong if they are helping someone be safe from a bad situation?) It was a question she would ask herself time and time again. Fearing someone would have traced her to a new town, she didn't mention her real name.

"I am visiting my aunt and uncle in Kansas City. They haven't met Charlie yet. I thought it would be fun taking the train trip rather than driving, but the bus trip was a little harder than I thought. I think the train might be more comfortable. I am so grateful she is sleeping with the movement of the bus. Maybe the train will help too."

"Even if you must wait for the train in Kirkwood, the station is pleasant enough. Volunteers operate the ticket booth. Your baby is adorable and quiet; my kids would have been screaming theirs heads off."

"I am lucky. Charlie has been an easy baby since her birth." Their conversation lulled as they got closer to St. Louis.

A stranger solved her problem by offering her a ride. The rest of the long trip was exhausting, although the baby slept with the bus motion. Emma read stories to her and showed her colorful pictures from books she had brought with her. She even walked up and down the aisle a few times so the baby could look around. She was shyly interested in the other passengers but didn't wave at them. They arrived in St. Louis a little ahead of schedule, but Emma wanted to go directly to the train station and wait for the next train headed west.

As they walked to Jane's car, they chatted like old friends. The drive through St Louis was fascinating! They passed a beautiful Ferris wheel with colored lights behind a majestic old train station. Emma was very appreciative that Jane did not ask her too many questions. Her little lies were piling up; as she told her, she headed to Kansas City and relatives. Jane was amiable and said it was easy to drop them off, as it wasn't too far from her home. The baby was starting to squirm in her car seat but was fascinated by the passing scenery.

The town of Kirkwood looked charming with its giant trees. It looked like a beautiful place to settle, but too close to a major city to be safe. So she decided to head west and chose a quiet little town in the middle of Missouri. She waved goodbye to the Good Samaritan as she went into the train station. Emma could tell it was old because it still had an emblem on the front for Missouri Pacific Railroad, which she knew didn't exist anymore. Instead, there were a few old pews lined up for waiting passengers. The train wouldn't leave for a while, so Emma decided to get a little snack from the vending machine. She had grabbed some coins from her jar at home, and now they were coming in handy.

It was strange to think about packing her backpack and suitcase in such a rush. Why had she included anything? She hoped she remembered underwear and other necessities. But, instead, she had packed diapers and baby treats.

She had a couple of hours before the train came into the station, which was plenty of time to change the baby's diaper and wash her face. Emma purchased a packaged sandwich in the machine and a bottle of water. Luckily, the supplies for the baby were holding out very well. She had just started eating real food. They walked up and down the station several times to pass the time. Emma let Charlie stand by the pews and hold on. Every day she was changing and growing up. They finally heard the train whistle from down the tracks.

The trainmaster was friendly as he handed her the tickets. She didn't need one for the baby. Emma felt much more relaxed as they were farther from her hometown. Lack of sleep was catching up with her, and she hoped she would sleep on the train for a few hours. This trip would be shorter than the bus trip, but Emma felt how hard it would be to stay alert, not knowing exactly where the train might stop. Finally, she might be able to close her eyes for a bit.

Even though she had just turned twenty-one the spring before, she felt much older. This past year has been challenging on so many levels. Emma had lost some of her carefree attitudes the year early. She had always been rather shy and afraid of doing anything to get attention. She remembered the old game, Truth or Dare, in school. Emma would never take the dare. Although not a dare, this trip was the craziest thing she had ever done. It was rather liberating, although leaving college was a difficult decision. Her parents were worried she might not go back to finish her teaching degree.

The train was comfortable, and there was more space for the baby to sit in the seat. Emma helped pass the time by rereading short stories with colorful pictures to the baby to keep her distracted.

As hours slipped by, the child stood by the train window and watched the scenery. She laughed when she saw a herd of cows in a pasture. Emma said, "That's a herd of cows… they go, 'Moo!" The baby started imitating the sound, "Moo." Several people around them started laughing at her antics. So much for attracting attention.

Town signs were passing by quickly, and Emma realized she needed to decide where to stop. They made several stops near Jefferson City to pick up passengers. As they continued west, she started thinking about where to stay. What would cause her to choose a town? It wasn't something she had planned ahead of time. She hadn't even looked at a map of Missouri. More importantly, no one could know where she was going. She kept watching the passing scenery, trying to figure out where to stop.

Charlie loved to watch the cows as the train passed so many farms. One town flashed by and then another. She knew she had to decide but was wary of which town would be best. Maybe something special would catch her eye and help her choose.

Then Emma noticed a big sign on the track advertising Hill Brook, northwest Missouri. The train was about thirty miles from the city limits. The billboard about the city had a few whirligigs surrounding it. She had read about them in a young adult novel called Whirligig. Her literature class loved the book, and she enjoyed her class's discussions about it. The whirligigs were spinning in the light wind as the train passed. They caused her to think about the little whirligig in her backyard, where the propeller turned a washerwoman scrubbing clothes. She wondered where whirligigs had originated and how hard they were to make. Any town with whirligigs sounded like a friendly enough town, so she asked the porter walking by if they made a stop at Hill Brook.

"Sure, do, little lady. Nice community, if I do say so. My aunt and uncle have lived there all their lives. I visit them often, and they love it. We will be coming up to the train station in about 45 minutes. I will make sure we stop there."

She gathered all of their belongings, and although it was late afternoon and dusk was approaching, she was hopeful she could find somewhere to stay, at least for the night. Then she would worry about the next day.

As the train slowed down, she edged her way through the aisle to the exit to the car, trying not to bump the baby carrier. Her backpack seemed heavier than when she started the journey. The porter was true to his word and waited for her at the door. When the train came to a complete stop, he helped her climb down the stairs. The train station was old yet painted a charming green with red accents. A man came out when he saw her and waved at the porter. "Hey Fred, making the last-night trip this time?"

"Last run of the day, which is always my favorite time because it's so quiet. You take care, Harry." And to Emma, as he set her suitcase on the platform and said, "Good luck, little lady and your baby. I think you'll like it here."

"Thanks for your help," Emma said as she stepped carefully onto the platform, adjusting the backpack once again. "Could you give me directions to get a bite to eat?" she asked the train station ticket master. "And could you put my suitcase in a locker for me? I will come back to get it tomorrow."

"I will be glad to store it for you." He handed her a claim ticket and said, "My neighbor, Nelly Blanding, owns the café near here. She let her grandkids name the place." He laughed, "Wait until you see the name. It makes everyone laugh. Just follow the street out in front and head down the hill. We are famous for our hills unless you are climbing them, and then they are infamous," the station manager said as he turned away. After picking up her suitcase, he continued chuckling and headed back inside.

The girl took the opportunity to look for a phone booth. Maybe a small town might still have them. Luckily, as she went around the train station's side, she found one on the building's corner, covered by an awning. She dialed the familiar number, waited for the ring, counted four times, and hung up. Then, feeling better after calling, she picked up Charlie and headed down the hill.

CHapter THree

…in which a perfect job falls in her lap

The following day pale sun streaming into the window woke the girl before Charlie. Emma stretched and relaxed back onto the pillow before she decided to get up.

Her feet touched the braided, homespun rug with pastel colors, but the cold tile felt cold as she tiptoed to the door.

She realized she still had on yesterday's clothes and had fallen asleep thinking about the long trip here. She forgot to go back down for tea and sign the register because she had fallen asleep. Emma hoped she could go to the shared bathroom before Charlie woke up. She still hadn't decided whether or not to use her real name. Maybe use her real first name, but a made-up last name. Luckily the door didn't squeak as she slowly opened it. Peeking up and down the hallway before she slid out the door, hoping she would not run into any other guests. She dressed in her best pants and a colorful turtleneck.

They only looked a little wrinkled, but she took them to the bathroom to loosen some of the wrinkles while showering. Her wardrobe was limited. Each of them only had a few changes of clothes, but Emma thought all towns had laundries. She remembered that she would need to pick up her suitcase at the train station to find a permanent place. The letter from her parents tucked in the inside pocket was essential to prove her identity.

The shower worked just fine, and the hot water and fresh-smelling soap made her feel better. She raced back to the room. She was glad she couldn't hear Charlie screaming. The place was quiet as she entered and checked on the baby. She was still sleeping. That would give the Emma time to get dressed before Charlie needed changing and clean clothes.

The only jewelry she had packed was tasteful and looked professional with the outfit. But, if she was lucky enough to find a want ad that might work for her, she wanted to look sharp. So, just as she was brushing her hair into a smooth ponytail, Charlie decided she had had enough sleep and was holding on to the crib's rails, shaking as if to say, "Get me out of here!"

"Good morning, Charlie," Emma said as she picked her up and cuddled her briefly before setting her down on the bed to change her and clean her up a little. "We will take a bath tonight; the old-fashioned tub in the bathroom will work. We need to move quickly with many errands to do today."

She noticed more about the boarding house; no, what was it? Bed and breakfast, the café waitress had said with a wink. It was lovely and clean. The staircase had black and white photographs with white matting and black frames. Some were photos from years before, but others were relatively recent. Emma was curious about who was in the pictures. Maybe if she could stay in the town, she could find out.

"Good morning," she said to the lady from the night before. She remembered her name was Millie. She was standing with a coffee pot at the kitchen door. There was a wooden highchair sitting by one of the chairs.

"Hello, again. Did you both sleep well last night? I figured when you didn't come back down. You must have been exhausted," she said as she put some pancakes on the tables. No one else had come to breakfast yet. It wasn't even eight o'clock.

"We both slept very well. I love the pillows."

"I order them specially. People have to sleep well to feel well, I always say."

"A philosopher, you are," Emma responded as she grinned.

"Sit down and have some pancakes. I found the highchair in the attic and cleaned it up for Charlie. That was her name, right?"

"Yes, that's it."

"I forgot to ask your name. You looked so tired; I thought you could use a good night's sleep."

The girl dreaded this moment. She hated lying, but there was no other choice. "So sorry, my name is Emma Morrison. I need to sign the registration book." She felt odd, lying about her last name, but at least she would write her actual first name.

"After breakfast is good enough. I warmed up the maple syrup, and the butter is soft. Help yourself to pancakes and bacon. Just the right meal for a cloudy morning in November." She turned toward the kitchen, then turned back and asked, "How long are you staying?"

It was a fair question, but Emma wasn't sure of the answer. "I'm not sure right now. I need to find a job and a place to stay for a longer time."

Millie thought for a minute and then said, "Let me think a bit about both.

I might have an answer for them."

"Do you have a local newspaper I could look through the want-ads for a job?"

"Sure do. It isn't much, but it does carry want-ads. Let me find a copy for you."

Emma watched the woman leave the room. The dining room was spacious, and the table had room for ten people. The wallpaper and the well-kept wooden trim were charming.

Emma cut up a pancake for Charlie and poured a little syrup over the pieces. Since spoons were still a challenge, Charlie used her fingers to pick up pieces of pancakes with syrup. After breakfast, she would be sticky, but Emma didn't care. Instead, she cut up a couple of sections for herself and took a bite. The pancakes were light and fluffy, and the syrup was warm.

Millie came back into the dining room with a folded newspaper. She handed it to Emma and said, "I have a friend who might have a solution. Let me call her and see if she can come over this morning."

Emma blinked, and she was fascinated that something could be happening to help her stay in this quaint little town far away from the situation she was trying to escape.

"Thanks so much, Mrs. Wilson."

"Call me, Millie. I have a feeling you might be staying around here. We need some young blood in this town. So many of us, especially on this street, is getting up in years and would love to see you and your little girl stay here."

"Why did you name your B and B after a flower?" Emma asked as she had been wondering about the name.

Millie looked wistful as she said, "It was my husband and my favorite flower. He died three years ago, so when I opened the B and B, I thought it would be a nice tribute to our long marriage."

Emma turned away and fussed a little with Charlie's food so that Mrs. Wilson wouldn't see the flush on her face. She had never been able to hide feelings as she remembered her parents' long, happy marriage.

Millie, her possible savior, left the room. Emma could hear her on the phone in the front parlor. The words were unclear, but she felt comforted by the older woman's concern and offered to help.

Charlie started to whine and wiggle, obviously finished with breakfast. "Hold on, little Miss, let me wipe your face and hands. Mrs. Wilson wouldn't like sticky hands all over her furniture. She is charming, but there are limits," Emma laughed as she tweaked Charlie's nose and lifted her down from the chair. The sweet decal of a teddy bear on the back of the highchair made her smile. She touched it gently, and somehow, it made her feel better than she had in a long time.

Charlie took off on her knees, crawling toward the front window and plants in pots.

"Wait. Charlie, let's find some of your toys from my backpack, and you can play in the living room."

As Emma was playing with Charlie, several boarders came downstairs for breakfast. The first was an older woman with pretty frosted hair, pleasant enough. She didn't say anything other than what a cute baby Charlie was. She had a decorative cane and walked carefully into the dining room. Right after her, an older man with totally white hair came down, sat in the chair by Emma, and tried to talk baby talk to Charlie.

He looked very dapper with his crisp white shirt and tweed sport coat. He had a neatly trimmed, totally white mustache and beard. She couldn't help but think that older men were so handsome with startling white hair. Emma smiled at him, and he introduced himself, "I am Walter. What are your names?"

"Hi Walter, I am Emma, and this is Charlotte, but I call her Charlie."

"Have you had breakfast?" he asked. "I am just about to have some."

"We just ate, and the pancakes were great."

"Millie is the best cook around. That's why some of us stayed so long time!"

"How long have you been with Millie?" Emma asked.

"Over a year. I retired last year and couldn't keep up with my home and thought it would be better to stay here than in a typical retirement home. It is nice to meet you. I smell Millie's great coffee, so off I go for breakfast."

"Nice to meet you, too."

He waved to Charlie, who smiled at him and moved her arms.

Emma heard more voices on the stairs and did a double-take at two older women who seemed identical. They even wore matching clothes. Emma smiled at them as they noticed Charlie chewing on her giraffe teething toy.

"What a cutie!" they said in unison. "I am Mary Margaret, and this is my sister, Esther Marie."

Emma introduced both herself and Charlie while admiring their adorable wardrobe. She had met more people today than she had in weeks. It was comforting to have conversations with friendly people. Emma couldn't help but ask if they were twins.

"No, but we are close in age, which we do not share with anyone," Mary Margaret teased as she smiled. "We love dressing alike, and it makes shopping easier for both of us. Most people we meet think that we are twins."

Another man came around the corner with a plaid blazer and carried a red hat. "Well, who do we have here?" he asked, looking at Charlie, who had stood up by the coffee table.

"This is Charlie, and I am Emma. We are staying here for a couple of days."

"Nice to meet you both. I am Monroe Jefferson, and I am ready for my pancakes. It must be my favorite breakfast around here. See you two later."

The rest of the morning slipped by quietly while Emma watched Charlie investigate her new surroundings. Each time the crawling little speed demon headed for a delicate treasure or a newfound interesting object, Emma would wisely distract her to something else.

When Charlie started fussing, Emma thought she must be tired from their long trip, so she took her up to the crib in the bedroom. Patting Charlie's head gently as she quieted down, Emma put a light blanket over her.

Emma's glance went to the window on the house's side, and she looked down the street. Did places like this still exist?

It was like a picture book with sidewalks and charming mailboxes. The houses were pretty close to the road, but yards were tidy, and some even had picket fences. Emma had always lived near New York City, like another world. Emma took a deep breath and felt a calmness overtake her. She felt even more relaxed than she had been for a long time.

Emma headed down the stairs thinking a coffee cup would warm her up. Instead, she left the bedroom door open so she could hear Charlie when she awoke from her nap.

As Emma came down the stairs, Millie answered the door. Emma had not heard the doorbell. An older woman with short white hair walked through the door with Millie. Her smile was warm and welcoming.

"Ah, here you are, Emma. I would like you to meet my friend, Olivia Williams."

Emma extended her hand to shake the woman's hand, and the woman did the same. Her hand felt so cold, but her smile was genuine and friendly.

"Glad to meet you, Emma. Goodness, it feels so nice and warm in here. The weather is colder today; I might even smell a little snow in the air. Millie, could I talk you into a cup of coffee? I brought my homemade coffee cake."

"Sounds wonderful!" said Millie, looking at Emma. "How would you like a cup?"

"I would love one," she said, covering up her curiosity about what Olivia Williams would suggest as a job.

"Coffee and the cake sounds delicious," Emma responded. She sighed quietly, thinking that she had found a little piece of heaven after such a difficult time in her life.

The other boarders had left for the morning. The two sisters were off to work on some Christmas preparations at their church. Then, both men were off to take their usual morning walk. It was so sweet that they all told her where they were going for the morning.

The women went into the cozy kitchen. They sat at a table that reminded Emma of a time long ago in her mother's kitchen. Millie put the coffee cake on a Fiesta plate. It almost brought tears to Emma's eyes as she remembered her mother's set of Fiesta china. The cups and saucers were different colors and looked great together. A few pieces even were chipped, but that made them even more enjoyable.

After a few sips of fragrant coffee and a bite of cake, Emma could no longer stand the suspense and blurted out, "Do you have an idea for a job for me?"

Mrs. Williams smiled and said, "I believe I do, Emma. My son is away, probably for another year, as a reporter in, well, I don't know where. He is moving around so much; he doesn't share where he is very often. He works for a cable news network."

"How does that affect me?" Emma asked.

"Well, he has a house near here. I am trying to take care of it but can't seem to manage it so well anymore. So I need someone to house sit and take care of it. I have the feeling you would be just right for the job."

Emma was stunned and asked, "You want me to live there and take care of the house?" It seemed like a dream come true.

"I would pay you, of course," Mrs. Williams added quickly.

"I can't believe you would trust a stranger to live in your son's house."

"Well, I have a hunch about you, Emma. You seem very trustworthy, and I suspect you need a place to stay and a job."

Emma felt her cheeks grow warm and knew she was blushing.

Before she could say another word, the three of them heard a cry from upstairs.

Charlie was awake and unhappy to be alone. "I will be right back," Emma said.

The two older women smiled at each other as if conspirators in mischief. Emma returned to the kitchen after she changed Charlie's diaper.

The baby turned her head to Emma's shoulder when she saw the two women in the kitchen.

"Maybe she would like some milk and a little cake?" Millie asked.

Charlie looked like a little princess with her court sitting in the old wooden highchair. She crammed the cake in with one fist and drank her milk in her Sippy cup with the other. All three women just sat and watched her playfulness.

"Well," Olivia asked, "what do you think about my offer?"

Emma looked away from the baby. "How can I ever thank you?"

"Maybe you better come over this afternoon and take a look at the place before saying yes. It is a large house. I will never understand why he bought it, as he is rarely here."

"Why don't you put Charlie down for her afternoon nap later and see the house after she wakes up. Do babies still take naps?"

"She does," Emma answered with a nod. Then, turning to Olivia, she suggested, "I can come over around two this afternoon. Would that work for you?"

"That will give me time to turn the thermostat up and take off some of the furniture covers."

Emma almost asked her son's name but was curious why Olivia hadn't volunteered it. She might know him from TV if he worked for a cable network. Maybe he was famous.

As the two older women started talking to each other, Emma had time to study them. She wasn't sure how old they were, but just their facial expressions showed a love of life and an interest in others' lives. Millie was a widow and thought maybe Olivia was also. She wondered how they dealt with death and went on with their lives. Emma was hoping to get to know them both better. Today was the first time in months, Emma felt like maybe her life wasn't going down the drain. She smiled, holding back tears, and all she could say was, "Thank you."

The women noticed her watery eyes and looked away.

chapter four

...in which Emma's life doesn't go down the drain

During Charlie's nap, Emma organized their belongings to move quickly if the job worked out. She sat on the side of the bed and patted the colorful quilt. It was a quilt made of old clothes, and the colors didn't match, but the pinwheel was charming. She looked closely and noticed all the tiny stitches that held the layers together.

She couldn't imagine anyone in her hometown involved with simple projects like quilting. Life seemed slower here than back home. Emma wondered if the church ladies around the town worked on quilts.

Emma realized that Charlie was standing up in the crib just looking at her, not crying or making any noise. "Hello, Peanut! Would you like to go on a short walk?" Not expecting an answer, Emma checked Charlie's diaper and changed her before leaving for the house.

As they came down the stairs, Olivia was waiting for them. She said they could walk, as her son's house was right around the corner.

"I am coming, too! I wouldn't miss this for the world," Millie called from the kitchen.

As they started walking, her curiosity was growing by the minute. What kind of home would a bachelor own, especially a man who traveled all the time?

The weather was chilly. Considering it was about two weeks before Thanksgiving, it was a pleasant and refreshing walk. As they turned the corner, Emma looked left and right, figuring out which home it might be. The street was quiet, but the day was so cloudy that the streetlights had come on, giving everything a glow. The houses were well tended. Many of the homes had wrap-around porches with swings. She sighed, just feeling comfortable on the street no matter which house it was.

Olivia pointed to the right and said, "It is the third house on the right. Its backyard is catty-corner to my backyard."

Emma thought she would have seen the house from the bedroom.

They walked up the steps to the front porch, which had rockers and a swing. It would be a beautiful spot to sit in the late afternoon in warm weather.

"Come on in," Olivia said as she opened the screen door and unlocked the door. "Unfortunately, I didn't have time to put up the storm door. I think I can get my handyman, Joe, to do that tomorrow. It will keep drafts from coming in the front door."

As the three of them walked in the door, the warm air felt comforting. "The furnace works well," Emma commented, taking off Charlie's coat.

She noticed a very comfortable home, as she looked around the large foyer, not too modern and not too old-fashioned. The living room was full of stuffed chairs and couches in front of a brick fireplace.

Mrs. Williams had turned on lamps throughout the first floor, making everything look warm and cozy. It was not a place you would expect from a bachelor.

"How long do you think your son will be gone?" Emma was mentally figuring out how she would plan the next few months.

"Well, last time I heard from him, he planned on being gone for at least a year. That was back in September when he was leaving New York. So I think it would be fair if I offered you a year's contract. That way, the house would be cared for and in good shape when he got back. He left me money to hire a house sitter and pay for upkeep. I just haven't taken the time to hire anyone."

Emma was stunned to hear she was being offered a job for a whole year. That would be a relief, and she wouldn't have to worry about having to move again. She liked this place and these two women.

Millie picked up Charlie as they walked around to the kitchen. Olivia and Emma followed. She noticed the dining room, which was right off the kitchen. There was a huge oak table with more than ten chairs around it. It would be an excellent place for a big holiday dinner.

"Your son loved to entertain?" Emma asked after seeing the table.

"Not really. Michael just liked the look of it."

The kitchen was amazing and looked modernized recently. Emma loved the black and white square tiles on the floor and the shiny white cabinets. The dishtowels were red checked and added a festive feel. Wouldn't it be fun to cook a meal in this kitchen, she thought to herself?

Olivia offered to take Emma upstairs to see the bedrooms and bathrooms while Millie and Charlie explored downstairs. Emma thought the carpeted stairs wouldn't be too much trouble, and she could get two gates to keep Charlie on the main floor or upstairs.

It wouldn't be too long before the baby could hurry up and down on her bottom. She had shown interest in standing up for a while but had been hesitant about taking steps.

"Which bedroom is your son's?" Emma asked as they entered the large hallway.

"He uses the one in the back for storing his clothes, although he hasn't done much decorating because he is gone so much. He left this September for somewhere in the Middle East, but I have had only a couple of emails from him." Emma thought Olivia looked sad for a second, but then she turned toward the windows.

"I love the front bedroom with the roofs and the corner nook overlooking the front yard. The previous owners left the furniture in some of the bedrooms. You could take that one near the bathroom, and the smaller room across the hall could be Charlie's. So, what do you think?"

"You have a gable window just like Millie's. It reminds me so much of my childhood home. I would love to take care of this house, and a year works out very well for me. Charlie seems comfortable, too."

"Why don't you sleep on it? Then, I can write up a contract and talk tomorrow morning. I am sure Millie will let you borrow the crib you are using at her house until we can find another one."

Emma felt as if she should pinch herself. Living in this home was too good to be true. They walked back downstairs, and she looked around as the two women played with Charlie, who was laughing happily. She pictured herself in the kitchen, making dinner and maybe inviting Millie and Olivia to thank them for their kindness. It had been a terrible year, and memories of it would pop into her head at the oddest moments. Maybe this opportunity would be the beginning of a new life. "I don't need to sleep on this decision, Olivia. I would be crazy to turn you down. I just remembered that I left my suitcase in the train station's locker because I couldn't carry it last night."

"Joe will pick it up for you," Olivia said

"That would be awesome. Do you think Joe will mind?"

"No, he does lots of odd jobs for me. But, he is very reliable." Millie grinned from ear to ear and gave Charlie a little hug. "We are going to have so much fun, Charlie. We all live so near to each other. We can have play dates," she said as she tickled Charlie, who laughed when the others laughed.

Millie, Emma, and Charlie waited while Olivia stayed to lock up and turn off all the lights. She left the porch light on so they could manage the steps. Emma turned and looked back at the house with a sad look, tears threatening to overflow onto her cheeks. She controlled them by blinking rapidly. The house had a charming appeal, and she was confused about why a bachelor would buy it to live there if he wasn't going to be around. But, on the other hand, she was thrilled to have a year to get her life in order.

CHAPTER FIVE

…in which Emma and Charlie get a place to call home

The next few hours went by in a blur as Millie made dinner. Emma used her time to pack Charlie's belongings, which didn't amount to much. Her things took up very little space in Emma's oversized backpack. Millie's handyman had picked up her suitcase at the train station, but she left it downstairs to take over to the house.

She sat on the edge of the bed and could hear Charlie downstairs, babbling her little language. Finally, the women were giving her the attention she needed. The long hours on the bus and the train were exhausting. She lost count of the hours. She felt so exhausted but encouraged by Olivia's offer of a job and a house.

There were so many secrets she held in her heart. She felt she would never survive. However, this offer would give some money and a place to live. She felt safer than she had in the past several weeks.

During dinner, the "twins" and the two gentlemen were so much fun, and the conversation around the table was lively. Emma had met most of the guests. One boarder had left earlier to meet a friend for dinner.

"Emma, this is my partner in crime, Monroe Jefferson. Did you meet him yesterday?"

"I did. Nice to see you again, Monroe! "Walter, what was your career before you retired?" Emma asked.

"I was a banker and was head of commercial financing. I can't say I miss it much. I miss the activity and the camaraderie with the other people in the bank and my clients. Retirement is wonderful in many ways, but I do miss some people."

Monroe spoke up right after Walter, eager to share his story. "I worked at Graham Construction Company as a plumber. The company owners were wonderful, and I miss them, but I don't miss fixing broken toilets." Everyone laughed at that comment.

Emma continued, "Mary Margaret and Esther Marie, are you both retired?

"We have been retired for about eight years. We taught Montessori, Mary as a teacher to fourth, fifth, and sixth graders, and I taught third graders. We miss faculty members and our students but run into them all over town, and that's fun."

They all were retired from professions but were not letting life pass. They were all looking for things to do for the holidays. They had interesting stories to tell and talked about what kept them busy now. They spoke about the Christmas Festival the town held every year. It sounded like everyone in the city was involved. Emma thought she might be able to help with some of the preparations. She had always enjoyed making things and decorating.

Thankfully, no one at the table asked her too many personal questions. She thought they might wonder why a young woman and a small child would be looking for work in a small town. But, instead, she was relieved and felt relaxed.

Charlie and Emma had breakfast with Millie and walked to the house around the corner the following day. Millie said that her helper had taken over an old playpen and highchair that Emma could borrow. Millie was going to ask Joe to bring the crib and her suitcase later that morning.

The sky was overcast, and it almost looked like snow again. Olivia had given Emma the front door key, so she turned it, cherishing the moment. She entered the hallway with a feeling of coming home, although maybe not to a forever place. It was at least a temporary home where she could settle her thoughts and have time to plan.

She put Charlie in the playpen between the kitchen and the dining room. Olivia had found it in her basement the day before. Emma took some time to look through the cabinets to know what to buy at the grocery store. She even noticed an old-fashioned butler's pantry with plenty of room for storage. She smiled when she looked in the refrigerator and found a casserole and a salad plus a milk bottle for Charlotte. Olivia or Millie must have brought them over earlier that morning. These two women were her guardian angels. Emma looked over at Charlie, who was contentedly chewing on her little giraffe teething ring. Everyone always thought she was a happy child.

She found a piece of paper and tried to think of items she would need to purchase. She only found a few canned goods, but the freezer had some food. The list grew as Emma thought of baby food. She was determined to invite Millie and Olivia for dinner. She thought she could get by on the money she had until Olivia paid her for the first week. Emma had the feeling that both of the women thought something wasn't quite right with a young woman and a baby on their own coming into a small town in the middle of November. She couldn't worry about that right now. She just needed to get through the year and then move on. No one would think to look for her in a little town in Missouri's northwest corner.

Emma was busy with many things to do and learn during the following week. The house was more to take care of than she expected. Emma still felt a little like a trespasser in someone else's home. She cleaned the owner's bedroom, which was a bit messy. She then closed the door to the room because she didn't want to be in his private place. The rest of the house had an old-fashioned feel but an updated kitchen, bathrooms, and lighting. After seeing some mail delivered, she remembered his first name was Michael. Emma took his correspondence to his mother, although she did not know where to forward it.

She had met the lovely couple, the Dolans, on the east side who had just retired the summer before. They had already adopted Charlie and Emma and even brought over some homemade blueberry scones. Pat and Dave Dolan reminded Emma of her grandparents with their energy and vigor. She often spotted them in their garden, cleaning up for the upcoming winter. They always talked to her and told her about the town and where to find things.

Walter, the dapper silver-haired man, walked over one day from Millie's to see how they were doing. Emma thought he could use activity in his retirement besides walking twice a day with Monroe. She would think more about that.

Mary Margaret and Esther Marie brought over some sugar cookies. Millie was generous in sharing her kitchen with her renters. They were hoping to get Emma involved in a project they had started after retiring.

Flora Kieffer, a florist in Hill Brook, donated flowers and supplies to make boutonnieres and corsages for the teens attending the homecoming dance. The cost of getting ready for dances could be overwhelming, and they thought it would be unique for the teens at the high school to have this support. Emma told Esther Marie and Mary Margaret she would be glad to help. They already had the list of the teens attending. They didn't want anyone to be left out.

The homecoming dance would be after the football game the Saturday before Thanksgiving.

"We will meet at Flora's Flowers on Friday before the dance after her shop closes, and we work during the evening making the boutonnieres and the corsages.

"That sounds like fun. You will have to teach me, but I love flowers. It is a very nice thing to do. I suspect money is always an issue for them. I have met some teens who have part-time jobs and heavy class loads. I admire them," Emma added.

The man next door who lived on the west side was a widower, and he even brought her his home-baked bread. It was still warm when he came over.

"Hello, I am Emma!" she said, welcoming him into the living room. Charlie was crawling right behind her but came to a dead stop and sat up and stared at the stranger.

"Well, hi, Emma, I am John Evans. I live right next door. Olivia just told me you were going to house sit for Mike this year. I would be glad if someone took care of my big old house. It was too much for Olivia to run back and forth to check on things and clean while he was gone. I understand you have met the boarders at Millie's B and B. She runs a great little place, I have heard."

"Please, sit down, Mr. Evans," Emma said, showing him a comfortable chair.

"Oh, please call me John," he said, wiggling his eyebrows at Charlie, who observed him.

Charlie laughed and started crawling over to his chair and pulled herself up by his chair's arm.

"Well, look at you go, girl. Someone is getting ready to walk!"

"Would you like a cup of coffee? I would love a slice of your bread."

"Sure! Smells good. You might find some strawberry jam in the cupboard. My wife used to give Mike several jars every year before she passed away."

Emma headed back to the kitchen through the butler's pantry, tucked away on the living room's far side. Sure enough, there were several jars of jam, just like he said.

She found a tray, put on two cups of coffee and several slices of his bread and the jam, and set it down on the coffee table. "I guess Olivia expects her son back this time next year."

"That young man never seems to be around for very long. He is some kind of correspondent with a cable network. It might be CNN. I think he is a pretty good writer and reporter. He must be over there in the Middle East somewhere, but I don't think Olivia knows."

Emma agreed with a nod as she handed him a cup of coffee. "She seems a little sad when she talks about him, but it could be that she just misses him. I feel a little odd staying in his house without him. But, on the other hand, I know she has been so nice to Charlie and me. This job was a lifesaver." She regretted saying that. She thought to herself, and I need to be more guarded in what I share.

"What is he like?" she asked to change the subject from her situation.

John didn't notice her a slip of the tongue and didn't ask what she meant. He said, "I have always liked Mike. We watched him grow up over the years. You can always judge a person by the way they treat their parents. He has always been helpful. I was sad when he closed up the house in September before leaving. I am so glad Olivia has hired you. The house seems alive rather than dark and closed because it had been closed for a couple of months. Olivia is lucky to have found you. I know she was worried about taking care of it for a year. Mike left money for lawn care in the summer and snow removal in the winter, but there is more to taking care of a home than that. I think Olivia just hadn't found the right person to live here."

Emma enjoyed listening to him talk as he was slathering his piece of bread with the jam. "This is so good," he said as he licked his lips. "Can Little Bits here have a small piece, Mom?" he teased.

"Sure! But you all are going to spoil her," Emma said, nodding.

"That's what we are here for," he said with his eyes sparkling.

Emma thought he might be a little lonely and loved to talk with people.

"What do you do in your retirement?"

"Have you seen the Harley Hardeman's Hill Brook Hardware Store down on Main Street? Harley heard that I have a woodworking shop in my basement and loved making things. So he asked me to make whirligigs for them to sell. It has become a pretty little industry. I have had a hard time keeping up with tourists' demands, especially for the holidays."

"You know, John, when you mentioned whirligigs, it made me think of a book I read in middle school, called Whirligig. I wonder if I could find it here at the city library, or is there a local bookstore?"

"Yes, there is a bookstore near the town square. A young woman named Elizabeth Turner opened it just this year."

"That's great. I will visit the library and the bookstore this week. I might read the book over again. Do you know the two men who rent from Millie—Walter and Monroe? Could they possibly help you with the whirligigs? They were just looking for something fun to do for the Christmas Festival. Do you think they could help you keep up with the orders you have?"

"That's a great idea, although I am not sure why I haven't met them. I know the two women who grew up in Hill Brook who live there. I just love to see them in their matching outfits. They have been active in many town events. They were teachers at the local public school, Avery School, but retired many years ago."

"Thanks for offering to work with Walter and Monroe. They would have no way to make things at the boarding house."

"I doubt she has a wood-making shop. I have all the equipment I need but could use more workforce."

"I actually would also like to learn how to make whirligigs. Maybe you could show me? "Emma paused and said, "I have another idea. What about coming over here for Thanksgiving dinner next week? I don't want to be alone, and I'm guessing you don't either!"

John didn't respond for a little bit, but Emma thought there were tears in his eyes.

He looked away briefly but then turned back to say, "That would be a great idea! What about asking Olivia and Millie? They would be able to bring some dishes to share. Maybe their boarders would like to come also."

"I love the idea. I will call Olivia and Millie right away." Emma clapped her hands in delight, and then Charlie did the same, losing her grip on the chair's arm. She fell with a bump and started to cry.

"Oh my, did you go bump?" Emma asked, scooping her up quickly and distracting her with her favorite toy. Charlie sniffled a couple of times and put her head on her shoulder. "Oh, I think you are ready for a nap."

Emma turned to John and said, "This will be so much fun. What do you think about having dinner on Thanksgiving Day around 4? That will give us time to cook everything and have a leisurely meal."

"Love the idea. I usually visit my wife's grave in the morning. What would you like me to bring?"

"What do you like to make?"

"I am famous for my sweet potato casserole with marshmallow topping. How does that sound?"

"It sounds delicious!" Emma felt the warmth of this man and was grateful for the chance to get to know him better.

CHaPTer SIX

...in which Emma meets many friendly people and one suspicious cop

During the week before Thanksgiving, the days seemed magical to Emma. The leaves had lost their color and had fallen quickly to the yards around the neighborhood. She had met Joe Hampton, the handyman, whom Olivia had hired for outside work. He had retrieved her luggage from the train station the day after she arrived in Hill Brook. He came over another morning to put on the storm door and take down the screen door. Emma thanked him for getting her suitcase and asked if she owed him something for his troubles. "No problem, Millie takes good care of me. She keeps me busy and always pays me."

Joe told her he would come back later that week to rake and bag the leaves. She said that she loved to rake leaves, and he could skip that week. He laughed and said, "I won't argue, as I have lots of other customers almost yelling at me to get their yards done."

"No problem for me, Joe. Please come back the week before Thanksgiving. I might not be able to keep it up, getting ready for homecoming and Thanksgiving."

"Thanks, Emma, and nice to see you again."

"See you around," she called to him as he got into his truck.

She loved the afternoon that she spent raking and bagging six-leaf bags while Charlie took her nap. The exercise felt terrific, and the weather was relatively mild. It was nothing like November in her hometown. She thought she smelled leaves burning, which she loved. No one ever burned leaves on the east coast, where she had grown up due to regulations. The city did provide bags for leaves, so she did fill a few bags. She paused with her chin on the rake head and just breathed slowly to relish the moment of peace.

Why had this all happened? It was pointless to ask that question, but she wondered about the feeling of uncertainty. Why had it worked out so perfectly? She could have run into real problems. Were there guardian angels for each one of us? She had so many questions.

She had called Olivia right after John Evan's visit to ask Olivia and Millie to come for Thanksgiving Dinner. She also mentioned the sisters and the two gentlemen boarders to see if they would like to come. Then, getting into the spirit, she invited the Dolans. This year, they were alone because their son, his wife, and their daughter would be traveling.

Everyone was thrilled and said they looked through their recipe books for dishes to bring. Mrs. Dolan wanted to bake two pies, pecan, and pumpkin, with whipped cream to go on top.

Luckily, Michael had a huge dining room with a large table when she added the extensions. There would be eleven, ten, plus one highchair. Maybe she would look around for a tablecloth to fit. She had gotten over her concern about snooping. After all, she was here for a whole year. She was beginning to think of him as just Michael. While she was standing there with her chin resting on the rake, a police car came down the street. She went back to raking, trying to ignore it. She didn't want them to ask any questions. Finally, they both got out of the patrol car and came over to talk to her.

"Hello, Miss, we are just checking on Michael's house while he is away. We went to school together. I am Josh Blanding, and this good-looking guy is my partner, Harrison Walsh. What's your name?" he asked with a friendly smile.

Emma didn't feel threatened because the officer seemed so friendly. "Mrs. Williams hired me to take care of Michael's house while he is away this year." She hoped that's all they wanted to know.

"What is your name, Miss?" Officer Walsh asked.

"Emma Morrison," she answered, hoping that would end the conversation.

"Where are you from?" he added, looking at his partner while he asked this.

"We don't need to know that. If Mrs. Williams hired you, that's all we need to know. So glad to know someone is taking care of the place," Josh said, looking at Officer Walsh with a frown. "You take care and let us know if you need anything."

Officer Walsh tipped his cap and walked to the car.

Officer Blanding smiled, nodding toward his partner, and said, "He is new and loves to ask questions. You have a nice day."

Emma pondered their visit, which had made her nervous. She wasn't sure if Phillip, her former brother-in-law, had hired a private investigator or not. A few people knew Emma had caught the bus in Salem, New Jersey, and not her hometown. She finished her raking and tried to forget the conversation. Emma had found herself looking at people with suspicion on the street and in town. She wondered if one of them might be a private detective looking for her. Emma had picked this town so randomly; how would anyone be able to track her down? She was second-guessing her decision to run away with Charlie. Her parents had helped her, but maybe they regretted her leaving so suddenly. She shook her head and went back to her raking.

After she piled the bags of leaves, she went back into the house. Her thoughts returned to Thanksgiving, and she had to be grateful for that.

Emma was determined to make the turkey and stuffing. She was excited to learn how to do it. She found a brand-new Better Homes and

Gardens Cookbook under the counter in the kitchen, written for a new cook. Emma spent some time looking at the instructions for roasting.

Earlier, while she had been cleaning, the memory of the book, Whirligig, crossed her mind. She thought she would go down to the public library sometime to see if they had the book.

CHAPTER SEVEN

...in which a walk-through town brings back memories

The next day, Emma and Charlie headed for the market. Charlie was sitting in her stroller with a big basket in the back. Emma was aware of her surroundings and watched for the police cruiser and other passing cars. She would be paranoid for some time. Would Phillip be looking for her? But then, her thoughts moved to happier things. First, Emma wondered if a fifteen-pound turkey would be enough for Charlie and ten people. Then, hopefully, the butcher would know.

Charlie loved being outside instead of cramped in the baby carrier as she had been during their trip. Emma decided to go on a walk around the town to get the feel of the community.

Although Hill Brook seemed small, there was a prosperous look to the business area. All the streets were swept clean, with no litter on the sidewalks. There were a few brick office buildings, and someone there was large pottery urns on each side of the front doors with all kinds of dried grasses and harvest flowers. Someone cared about the professional look of the buildings but made them look appealing at the same time.

She noticed a little pet store near the next street corner with a golden retriever statue guarding the front door. It was called the Bark around the Park Pet Store. Emma thought that there must be a lot of pets in Hill Brook to require an independent pet store. She stopped and looked in the front window display of cute collars and leashes. Tears popped up quickly. She also chuckled over the memory of her and her sister, Susie, when they were younger.

They played in the backyard with their dog, Charlie Brown, who dragged his leash around the fenced-in yard one summer morning. He loved to run around like crazy. He was an energetic wirehair terrier. The way he pulled the strap around made both of them laugh. Susie, older than Emma, decided it was time to play dog and walker, so she grabbed the leash, took off Charlie Brown's collar, and put it around Emma's neck. They both laughed as Emma crawled around the backyard with the collar and leash held. The dog raced around them, barking as if he wanted his collar back. They both fell on the ground laughing when their mother called from the kitchen window, "What are you doing? Take that collar off from around Emma's neck. You two are going to drive me crazy this summer!"

It wasn't until Charlie bounced up and down in her stroller that Emma returned to the present time. What a funny memory, but it also made Emma feel sad. She thought to herself, did I enjoy those times as much as I should have? Then, shaking her head, she pushed the stroller down the street.

She was feeling more comfortable now, even though some things brought back memories of her sister from their childhood. Each small business along the main street had a personality, like the pet store.

People walking by were stopping and talking to Charlie. A baby was always a magnet to all types of people. Everyone was friendly, and many introduced themselves. Finally, Emma felt safe enough to talk to these people. She looked across the street at a charming shop with a festive green striped awning above the front window and door. The inside window display had a pretty white silk wedding gown. Formal wear and wedding dresses reminded Emma of another memory flooded back to Emma of Susie's wedding day. It was the prettiest day in June, with a deep blue sky. The wedding party had to walk across a busy street in town to the old church. All the cars stopped to watch Susie and her bridesmaids walk across. Everyone was smiling and laughing. Emma had been holding up

Susie's train so it wouldn't get dirty or wrinkled. What a great day it had been. Shaking her head, Emma continued walking down the street to get to the library to find Whirligig.

It seemed fitting to reread that book after hearing about actual whirligigs for the past weeks in Hill Brook. She might even check out a book about how to make them. She figured they would be challenging to make with the motion of the propeller and the moving parts. She hoped John would show her how to make them.

As she walked around the town, she realized that Hill Brook had many interesting people and businesses. The storefronts were welcoming. Emma thought that meant that the shop owners must work together. The people here seemed to walk slower. No one rushed around the town. The decorations for Thanksgiving festooned each lamppost, and there were bales of hay around the Hill Brook City Hall.

She found the library near the park and went through the front door. She thought to herself, is there any better smell than books? So she went to the main desk and asked for the young adult section. An older man working on a computer referred her to the checkout desk. She also wondered if someone could look up the book's author, Whirligig. Emma thought it was Paul somebody, but couldn't remember.

"Hi," Emma said to the young woman behind the checkout desk. "I am new to town but wondered if I could check out a book under another person's name."

"What is the name?" the librarian asked.

"Michael Williams. He lives on Lynchester."

"Oh, of course, I know Michael. I didn't know he had gotten married and had a child."

"Oh no, I am house-sitting for him while he is in the Middle East. His mother, Olivia hired me," she added.

"Let's do that, and if you intend to stay in Hill Brook, you can get yourself a card."

"I am Emma; what is your name?"

"My name is Amy Perkins. I am so glad to meet you. How do you like Hill Brook?"

"Everyone is so friendly."

"Let me look up that book on our computer. I remember reading that book when I was in school. The author is Paul Fleischman. It will be under the author's last name in the stacks, right over there," she said, pointing to the bookshelves to the right. "It is about the consequences of our actions and moving beyond tragedies," she said.

Emma walked along the shelves, searching for F. When she found that, she had to lean down to see if they had Whirligig. She was excited to see the book and pulled it out of the shelf. It seemed like Amy would let her check it out under Michael's name.

"How long have you been the librarian in Hill Brook?" Emma asked Amy.

"I came back to town because my mother told me that the long-time librarian had retired. I have wanted to be a librarian ever since I was a little girl. Books have been my lifeline all my life. So I applied and took the job. They gave me two weeks to pack up my apartment in Kansas City and move back. I went to high school here and just feel more comfortable in a small town."

"I know what you mean. Charlie and I moved here a short time ago, and we love it.

"Have you ever met Mike Williams?"

"No, just his mother, who hired me. She thinks he will be gone about a year or so."

"I went to high school with both Mike and one of his best friends, Josh Blanding, but I haven't seen either one of them yet. Then, however, I heard that Josh had become police chief of Hill Brook.

"I wonder if he has a library card?" Emma said, laughing. "If not, we will have to get him one! I'm so glad you had this book. It was one of my favorites in school. I have meant to reread it since I heard so much about whirligigs for the Holiday Festival in town."

Amy handed her the book and said, "I heard that John Evans had made quite a few sales. So I might buy one for my parent's garden. The designs are charming, and I love that whirligigs use the wind to work. I had one in my backyard when I was growing up. It would be fun to learn how to make one."

"I know what you mean about the charm of the whirligigs. Please wait until you see the stylish patterns they have made for the whirligigs they sell at the festival. They assemble tents for vendors and crafters in the town square near the city hall. They have fireworks on the first night of the Holiday Festival, two weekends before Christmas. I love fireworks, so we are closing the library a little early that day to attend. By the way, we check books out for two weeks. Is that enough time for you?"

"That will be plenty of time to reread it. Thanks so much."

After Emma signed out the book under Mike's name, she headed toward the door. She wondered if Amy, Josh, and Michael had a history together. It was fun to wonder if they had ever dated.

Emma thought this was at least the second person she had met near her age. She was happy that this town had different generations still living there. She and Charlie left the library with the book. Charlie had fallen asleep while they were in the library and looked comfortable enough. Emma loved walking around the streets in Hill Brook. She turned down another road and noticed a small storefront next to a gelato store. It was impressive that someone from here had learned how to make gelato. Some people she knew in the East had gone to Italy to learn how to make it.

It looked as if the bookstore with the small storefront was not too busy right now. Emma peeked through the front window and then glanced at the name on a board over the window. It read, "The Paige Turner." Emma smiled at the title and wondered who had named it. It had to be an independent bookstore, just one more surprise for a small town.

"Hello," she called as she entered and saw someone behind the counter. There were many books, but the best part was a small fireplace with comfortable chairs. It would be nice to have somewhere to sit and read for a while.

"Welcome to my store. I am Elizabeth Turner, and I just opened the store last month. It's so nice of you to stop by."

"I love the name of your bookstore."

"My middle name is Paige, so I thought the play on my name would be fun. I wanted to promote reading and writing in Hill Brook. I hope to encourage them to write down stories of their ancestors and their childhood histories. The people in this town love to give their businesses interesting names. Have you seen the hardware store? Harley had fun with that name. So sorry! I am rambling, but I'm just so glad to have someone stop by. It is hard to get a business running. Are you looking for a particular book?"

"I just went to the library and found it there. So I picked up a copy of *Whirligig* by Paul Fleischmann. I wanted to read it because the town has a reputation for selling whirligigs. Do people come from all over to buy them?"

"We have lots of visitors coming to the Holiday Festival. They come from both Kansas City and St. Louis. It's so good for our economy."

"Being in your bookstore reminds me of the book discussions we had in school. The teachers would start with a question, and all of us would just discuss books from our point of view. It was called the Socratic type of questioning. I liked that we could disagree but do it nicely. I think it taught me how to think for myself," Emma remembered.

Elizabeth nodded and said, "Some young adult books have intriguing and interesting themes. I wonder if some of the kids in the middle school would be interested in discussing books. We have book clubs for adults in town but haven't thought about teenagers. I think kids might be able to dig down into the themes of the books they read."

"Do you have a book club for people in my age group?"

"We do, and I even started a group for toddlers. I read and show them picture books. That has been the most fun. I bought a princess hat to wear, and they call me The Reading Lady."

Emma laughed and wondered if Charlie would come to Elizabeth's reading group. "Do you think Charlie is old enough to come to your Story Time?"

"I think it is short enough and I show lots of pictures. Parents usually hold the children on their laps. Sometimes we make hand motions. The parents help them understand what we are doing. Our next "Reading Lady" is on the day after Thanksgiving. I usually do them on Friday mornings when the kids are not quite ready for their naps."

As Emma was about to leave the bookstore, she saw Joe Hampton pull up in front of the building and enter the bookstore. "Hi Joe, what's going on today?"

"Hi, Emma! Fancy meeting you in a place like this," he said, winking. "And who is this charming Miss?" patting Charlie on her hand.

"That's Charlie, and she's about 14 months old."

"Just checking on one of my last building projects for Elizabeth. I built her a new checkout counter. The one here for the previous tenant was almost ready to collapse.

"So, being a handyman for Millie is not all you do."

"I do a little bit here and there. I like to keep busy." He turned to face the owner and said, "Hi Elizabeth, how is the counter working out? Do you like the pull-out drawer for wrapping paper? I thought that it would be easy to store paper and then wrap it right there."

"I love the drawer and especially the beautiful wood on the top. You are a masterful craftsman," Elizabeth said, admiring the countertop.

Emma was sure Elizabeth was blushing. An exciting development, she thought to herself. "See you soon, Elizabeth, and nice to see you, Joe."

"Thanks for the information about the toddler storytime. See you soon." She heard the little bell above the door when she left the bookstore. Could this town get any cuter?

Emma paused as she pushed Charlie out the door and looked back as Joe and Elizabeth stood talking for a while.

After wandering around town that morning, Emma decided to go back 'home' as Charlie would need a nap after lunch.

That afternoon went by quickly as Charlie fell to sleep after getting home. Emma used her time to clean a little for the holidays. She had invited quite a few people for Thanksgiving, and she might even do more entertaining during the Christmas holidays. Her parents used to have an open house on Boxing Day, after Christmas Day. In England, it was an old tradition where the servants came to the festivities. Emma's mother always had loved that holiday as she enjoyed reading historical romances.

CHaPTer EIGHT

...in which Emma spreads her wings at Molly's Market

E mma realized that it was a little less than a week before Thanksgiving, and she needed to go to the market in town. So after Charlie woke up from her afternoon nap, they went to Molly's Market, the only grocery store in Hill Brook. She had heard it was different from the big superstores in her hometown. It was so funny how business owners in Hill Brook loved to use alliteration in their business names, like the hardware store.

Emma was going to purchase some of her Thanksgiving ingredients, although not the turkey. She wanted to wait to buy a fresh turkey, which her mom had done every year. As she walked the few blocks to purchase Thanksgiving dinner ingredients, she passed by Harley's Hill Brook Hardware Store. Emma couldn't wait to meet Harley, but that would wait for another day. The windows were decorated for harvest time, displaying several charming whirligigs. Each one was more interesting than the next with a unique personality. If John had made even some of them, he was very creative and skilled. She hoped that the Bed and Breakfast residents would be interested in helping John with his creations. Even if they had no natural woodworking talent, they could sand pieces or help John assemble. Emma grinned at the displays of whirligigs. Maybe she could buy one for Olivia to thank you for the job.

The town market was as appealing as the diner where she ate that first night. It was nothing like the large grocery stores back East, which could be overwhelming. It was small but well-stocked. The first thing she saw was a display of mums and all kinds of autumn bouquets. She thought she had to have a centerpiece to make the table seem festive. The holiday table needed candles. Memories of her childhood holidays started coming fast and furious. Her family had enjoyed Thanksgiving almost as much as, if not more than Christmas. They loved just spending time with each other without the pressure of gift-giving. Only the memories of a fire in the fireplace and eating popcorn from a large tin were enough. There were always three kinds: plain, cheese, and caramel. She and Susie usually fought for the caramel and cheese.

Emma shook her head to stop the memories and reminded herself to pick up a big can of popcorn next week. Then, she could share with her Thanksgiving guests. That would be a happy memory. Also, she thought that she needed to create new memories.

Crackers and cheese appetizers would be just enough and not too much before the Thanksgiving meal. Millie was bringing her homemade apple cider and some local sausage. Emma's stomach started growling right then, just thinking about it. The planning for dinner is so much fun, she thought to herself. Charlie was having a great time looking at all the items for sale. Luckily, she couldn't reach any of them.

As Emma passed the bakery counter, the young woman behind it asked if Charlie could have a cookie. Emma smiled and said, "Sure! How nice of you. Maybe not chocolate, but a plain sugar cookie would be great!"

Charlie grinned with her two bottom teeth showing proudly. She giggled as she bit into the soft cookie. "How cute she is; what is her name? My name is Charlotte McManus."

"Oh my, small world, her name is also Charlotte, but we call her Charlie," Emma answered.

"Are you and your husband new in town?" asked Charlotte.

Emma paused for a moment and then said, "We are by ourselves. My name is Emma."

The girl wisely thought not to pursue the answer. "Well, welcome to Hill Brook. Where are you staying?" thinking that was not too much to ask.

"We are housesitting over on Lynchester at Michael Williams' house while he is overseas."

"Interesting, I wondered because I have passed his house a few times and noticed there were no lights on for a few weeks. I hadn't seen Olivia in a while, so I didn't know about her son. I love her."

"Wow! Everyone knows everyone in a small town," Emma said, laughing. "We love her already. She is a wonderful lady. Well, I am off to order a fresh turkey for Thanksgiving. My first," she admitted.

Charlotte winked at her. "You will do great. I have some wonderful dried bread to make the stuffing. Would you like to order some? You will also need celery, onion, and seasonings. Do you have directions?"

"I brought the recipe for stuffing with me. I am making a 15-pound turkey, I think. I am heading toward the butcher counter right now. Do you know how much bread I will need?"

"Sure do. I have been making bread stuffing all my life. My grand-mother taught us how. Would you like to order several dry loaves? Something about Thanksgiving makes me feel so sentimental. How about you?"

Emma paused before answering, "I know what you mean. Memories are strong this time of year. Thanks for the information about the stuffing and turkey. I guess it is too early to pick a fresh turkey now."

"Why don't I just take your order, and you could have it delivered with the turkey since you are ordering a fresh turkey?"

"That's just what I was doing next. Thanks for the suggestion."

Charlotte turned to pick up the ordering pad, and just as she looked up, a young man came up next to Emma and said, " Could you spare a cookie for a brave police officer?"

Both Emma and Charlotte turned and looked at the man who asked. "I think that I can provide a cookie for you. Are you new to Hill Brook, sir?"

"I am. I just finished training, joining Josh and his crew this week. My name is Harrison Walsh. It is nice to meet you, Charlotte. Can I call you Charlie?' he said, laughing.

Charlotte looked at him and said, "Can I call you, Harry?"

"I think not," he said, laughing also.

Charlotte winked at Emma and said to Harrison, "Have you met Emma? She is housesitting for Olivia Williams's son."

We did meet the other day while you were raking leaves. "Hi, Emma." He didn't know who Mike Williams was, but he said, "We both are new to town then, I guess."

"Nice to see you again." Emma didn't think he was so suspicious as that day.

Charlotte handed him a giant sugar cookie; the bakery was famous for baking these big cookies. He took a bite and had to wipe off all the sugar from his lips. "I think I can go on today. This cookie is the best. Thanks." Harrison tipped his cap to both of them and walked off.

Emma turned to Charlotte and said, "Well, wasn't he funny? I think you must have an admirer, Charlotte."

"Oh, I don't know. Harrison may be back for more cookies, but not just for me." They both laughed as Charlotte wrote the order Emma placed for dried bread.

Emma decided to purchase some fresh spices suggested by the Better Homes recipe. The butcher was equally friendly as everyone at Molly's. He took her order for a fresh turkey. "Do you need this delivered the day before Thanksgiving? My delivery boy could run it over that morning."

"That would be great!" She could take some of the ingredients with her today. As she placed more purchases in the basket, she noticed Charlie had fallen asleep.

Emma realized her money was holding out well as she paid for her items. Michael's kitchen had some food, and the freezer was packed. Olivia encouraged her to eat the food. If he left for the whole year, much of it would be outdated. Funny, she kept calling him Michael or Mike even though she had never met him. She thought she would probably be gone before he returned next year.

During the walk home, she noticed the temperature was dropping, and the wind was picking up. She was glad to get back to the warm air inside and settled Charlie down for the rest of her nap. The week before, she had spent going through the house, dusting, and cleaning the bathrooms, which Olivia had mentioned would need some attention first.

The kitchen also needed some cleaning, but she didn't need to reorganize supplies for the most part. It seemed odd that a bachelor who was rarely at home would ideally remodel a house. It was too early to ask Olivia about her son. Emma wasn't sure about their relationship and had more questions than answers. She didn't want to pry into this man's life, especially since she didn't want them to pry into hers. It was intriguing the way one life can mirror another.

Her conversation with John about whirligigs and how he made them in his basement workshop had been exciting. Emma was so glad he could stay productive. She recalled the men who lived at the B and B and wondered if they would help John.

However, she felt that living in a boarding house could be restrictive in creating projects.

While drinking tea, she relaxed, reviewing the directions for stuffing and roasting the turkey. She remembered her mother always made oyster stuffing every Thanksgiving, which gave it a slightly rustic flavor. No one in the family liked it, but no one wanted to hurt her mother's feelings by not eating it.

Memories are more potent this time of year, she thought, recalling that conversation with Charlotte at the bakery counter. She was determined not to be sad but to be optimistic about the future. Home did seem far away, but she had to remain where she was, no matter what. Her secret was safe here, in a little town in Missouri.

Just then, she heard the doorbell. It was Pat Dolan from next door. It is nice having friendly neighbors on both sides of Michael's house. John Evans had been so supportive and kind.

"Hi Pat, come in please," Emma noticed a pan of something in Pat's hand, and she was curious about what she had brought.

"I brought you a little gooey butter cake to tide you over until I bring the pies for Thanksgiving."

"How sweet of you. Someone told me St. Louis was famous for gooey butter cake."

"I grew up in a suburb of St. Louis, Kirkwood, and we often went to Kirkwood Bakery for the cake."

Emma almost said that she had transferred to the train at the Kirkwood Train Station but wisely decided it was best not to mention. Instead, she asked, "When did you move here?"

"I met my husband, Dave, at the University of Kansas, and we compromised by living in between Kansas City and St. Louis. We both love small towns, and Hill Brook is a great place to have a family."

"I have only been here for a few weeks, but I love the people. Maybe the time of year is part of it."

"I know what you mean. I also have a favor to ask about Thanksgiving. Our granddaughter, Ella Rose, stays with us while her parents take a business trip for two weeks. They decided that she wouldn't go with them on the trip to Europe, and she was not too happy to be stuck here. They just emailed that they won't make it home until after New Year. We should enroll her in Truman Middle School so she doesn't get behind. They live in Kansas City, and our small town does not provide her with enough things to do. I thought maybe she would love to see Charlie and play with her on Thanksgiving. Would that be okay? I know you would have a full house."

"That would be great fun. How old is your granddaughter? Charlie will love the attention."

"She is thirteen," Pat answered.

Emma invited Pat to share a piece of the cake and brewed two cups of tea. She had never had friends at her grandmother's age, but she enjoyed meeting Millie, Olivia, and Pat. They were all young-looking women.

"How are you settling into Mike's house? I hated seeing it so dark while he was gone. I have the feeling it was too much for Olivia to take care of two homes. She is very energetic for her age, but that was too much. Mike was upset before he left and wasn't thinking clearly."

"Olivia told me that he was upset that his fiancée canceled their engagement and wedding because he was going overseas for an extended tour with a cable network."

"I heard the same thing, but I am so glad that she found you. An angel dropped from heaven right at her doorstep. Millie saw your potential when you came to her door."

"I felt like those two ladies were my saviors. I wanted a job, but to get a place to stay and a job all in one was too amazing." She hesitated in saying anything else, but she didn't want to be too mysterious either.

"The cake is wonderful, but I better not overeat it. I have to save room for your pies. John has told me they are fabulous."

"He is a dear. Do you know he is famous around here for making whirligigs? You should see his workshop. It is like a magical place with painted wood everywhere."

"I was thinking about buying one of his creations to give to Olivia for Christmas to thank her for hiring me."

Just then, they both heard chattering from upstairs and laughed. "Is Charlie always that cheerful waking up? My children were never that calm when they woke from a nap."

"She is a pretty easy-going baby… although she is getting so big so fast, I may have to call her a toddler pretty soon. A few months ago, we were a little concerned that she seemed underweight for her age group, but our doctor said she was within the weight range for a year old. She still loves her naps four months later, which is great for all of us." They both laughed when Emma said that.

"They do grow up fast, but hopefully, you can enjoy every day with her."

Emma thought the comment was very prophetic; she would treasure every day with her. Pat let herself out quietly so Emma could go upstairs to pick up Charlie. Emma thought walking this tightrope would get more complicated with these beautiful people. Lying even for a good reason was difficult for Emma. She tried to avoid attention by not opening a checking account. She thought she was safe. She had no idea her peaceful life would soon be disturbed.

Chapter Nine

*...in which Hill Brook citizens show
Emma the magic of belonging*

A t the end of the week, Emma got a call from the bookstore owner, Elizabeth Turner, who said she had been thinking about their conversation. "I can do a book discussion for the teenagers, but what about having them come to a writing club? It might encourage them to write about their thoughts without the pressure of grades."

"What a great idea!" said Emma, "I'm sure they write in school, but maybe they would like to share their thoughts in stories about their lives. We could do personal narratives, especially stories of their childhood. They might enjoy sharing stories."

"Do you know anyone in middle school?" Elizabeth asked Emma.

"This would be perfect for the Dolans' granddaughter, Ella Rose, who is here visiting. She might enroll in Truman Middle School, as her parents may not be home before New Year's. Enrolling in school could help her fit in with the group."

"Could you ask her if she has met anyone who might like to join a writing club?"

"I will talk to her. Do you have supplies for a writing group?"

"I can order some journals and have them shipped overnight."

"Could you order one for me? I have a little notebook I write in now."

Elizabeth smiled at Emma. "I am so glad you came into my bookstore and suggested such a great way to get the teens together to share their stories. It might be fun to have our town whirligig maker come to tell the kids about his life and why he got involved with making whirligigs. What caused him to start making whirligigs? They are very unusual. We could all could see how he develops the process."

Emma nodded and said, "Great idea. I will talk to both Ella Rose and John."

Later that day, Emma called Mrs. Dolan to ask if Ella Rose was enrolling at Truman while her parents were overseas. Emma told her about the writing club and wondered if she thought her granddaughter might be interested.

Mrs. Dolan told Emma, "She loves to write and has taken to a little diary I bought her. It sounds like a writing club would be perfect for her and might help her meet some teens her age. We will go over to the school to talk to the counselor. Her school in Kansas City said they would fax her records so the counselor could place her in the right classes."

Emma was thrilled and said, "Thanks for asking her. I guess we would need eight or so. Having both boys and girls would make discussions more interesting."

"I will give you a call when I talk to Ella Rose and the counselor. He may have some ideas of whom to ask about joining a writing club outside of school," Pat said.

"Thanks, I will talk to you before Thanksgiving," Emma answered, excited that Ella Rose would be staying.

Later that day, Emma received a call back from Pat, who put Ella Rose on the phone. She was so excited about registering at the local middle school. "I met a bunch of kids my age, and I was telling them about the writing club at The Paige Turner."

"How many journals do you think we need to order? I can look up the price on Amazon, or Elizabeth can check with her supplier. I will let you know the cost, but I guess it will be under $10. How does that sound? By the way, what time is school out in the afternoon?"

"I think there were eight kids plus me who were interested. Some of them might bring their laptops for writing. I like to use a pen or pencil, too, though. Let me check the schedule they gave me about the time to start. It says buses arrive at 2:45 pm, and walkers leave before that. So we start school at the crack of dawn here."

"I will tell Elizabeth that you could make it by 3:30 next Monday. The journals should be in by tomorrow, and they can purchase them at the bookstore. She ordered a journal for me, too. I will bring cookies to give you all a snack before the session."

Emma immediately called Elizabeth with great news about ordering enough journals. She told her they could pick them up Friday afternoon if she thought they would be in by then.

"I will call right now, and they can overnight them for me. I'm so excited about having this writing club."

"I love to write stories and will be ready to join the group myself."

"Sounds great! I will call you when the journals are delivered, but I think they will be here tomorrow morning."

Emma called Olivia right away, wondering if Charlie could come to stay with her so Emma could attend the writing club.

"No problem, Emma, I would love to have her. Just having you take care of Michael's house has freed up my days. I was trying to get over there at least once a day."

"And I love it! Thanks again for your help."

That Friday was picture-perfect autumn weather. Emma was able to take Charlie to the little park near Michael's house. Ella Rose had been sitting on her grandparents' front porch, wrapped in a blanket, reading a book when Emma left for the park. Emma was glad to have ordered a journal for herself. She thought of several story ideas to write.

Right now, she was still worried about being followed. Reality intruded now and then, and she would look at cars driving by just in case someone had followed her to Hill Brook. However, she had not seen the black car after that first time.

She put Charlie in a toddler swing on the playground because she loved the attention. Several girls at the park asked if they could push her. Emma stayed close and pulled a notebook out of her handbag to jot down some ideas of things in her childhood. She had lots of fun stories of her family she could share. She would be ready to help the teens brainstorm before Monday. Emma was already planning what to bring for a snack.

Maybe they would be willing to schedule talks each Monday after school. Elizabeth and Emma could ask them. They could finish their stories by the start of the winter break from school. Although Charlie wasn't ready to leave the girls pushing her, Emma thanked the girls and went to head to Olivia's.

She was grateful that Olivia and Millie were willing to watch Charlie so Emma could help Mary Margaret and Esther Marie with the flowers for the homecoming dance at the high school.

As Emma entered the florist shop, the fresh, refreshing smell of the flowers overwhelmed her. All the fragrances seemed to meld together and become beautiful. She was sure that roses were part of it. The owner came out of the back with large containers of different flowers.

"Hi, there!" the woman said, "I am Flora Kieffer, the owner of Flora's Flowers. Welcome! "

Emma couldn't help but chuckle over the clever use of alliteration.

"Hi, Flora, I think I beat Mary Margaret and Esther Marie. They should be right behind me. I am so excited to help with the flowers for the teens!"

"It is fun for me also! I always have fresh flowers, and I am glad to donate some of them for the teens." Their parents have lots of expenses for these parties and dances. So making the corsages and boutonnieres is one way we can help them."

"I hope you can show me how to make a nice corsage. I have never done it before."

"Well, I have made the little bows already to get ahead. We will put the finished corsages in plastic bags and keep them in the refrigerator here at the store until tomorrow. Then, the boys and girls pick them up during the day. I'm glad a few townspeople offer donations to help cover the cost. Also, older residents attend the dance as chaperones to give the parents a break. Plus, that gives their teens a break from their parents. So sometimes I help out to chaperone and take a date," she added, blushing a little.

Emma smiled but didn't ask who that was. She already wondered if she had met someone, she could introduce Flora to. "It's a beautiful idea to go to the dance, and it makes me love this town even more than I already do."

"Let me show you how to twist the wire and floral tape around the roses. Or please take off the thorns from the roses first. You have to be careful not to hurt your fingers. I think the ladies have a list of specific colors of the girls' dresses. We want to match the corsages to their dresses as best we can. I have lots of white roses, which will go with anything. I also ordered extra mums to go with the harvest theme."

Just about then, Mary Margaret and Esther Marie came in the door carrying a notebook. Emma learned it had all the names of the girls and boys ordering flowers.

"Hello, Emma and Flora! We are ready to report for duty. Flora tells us what to do."

"I have already asked Emma to remove thorns from the roses to wrap them in floral tape."

The boutonnieres were easier to make than the corsages. Flora kept track of the colors as the three women did the jobs she assigned to them. The four women worked well together, and the hours passed quickly. Emma finished the evening by placing the flowers in the plastic bags and securing each with a long pearl pin. They looked so pretty. Mary Margaret was happy to put names on the bags. The boys would pick up the girls' corsages, and the girls would pick up their dates' boutonnieres.

They finished around 9:00 pm, and Flora put flowers into her large refrigerators. Mary Margaret and Esther Marie agreed to help distribute the flowers Saturday. "That is the most fun to see the teens with their flowers," added Flora.

"Thanks for asking me to help with this!" Emma said as she swept up the floor of all the stems and the wire they had cut. "I loved learning about flowers and especially how to make corsages."

Emma spent the weekend either playing with Charlie or reading Whirligig. She also cleaned the house for Thanksgiving dinner. Emma had bought everything except the fresh turkey and dried bread, which she ordered delivered the day before the big day.

CHAPTER TEN

...in which Emma loves being a neighbor

On Monday morning, Emma woke up excited about the writing club. She remembered that she wanted to buy flowers and candles for the dinner table for Thanksgiving but could do that on Tuesday or Wednesday. Emma glanced around the dining room and pictured everyone sitting there. She had found the extensions to the table. They were easy to add. She might need one more but would wait until she knew everyone was coming. The china in the cabinet was beautiful, and Emma wondered if it had been an engagement gift. She counted chairs and figured out where everyone would fit. Charlie would be in the highchair on the corner and John at the head because he had agreed to carve the turkey.

Suddenly, she remembered the one woman who stayed at the boarding house but had not introduced herself. Emma wondered if she might like to come to dinner. She didn't even know her name.

"Come on, Peanut, let's take a walk over to Millie's house and see if we can find out about the mystery woman we didn't meet."

Emma carried Charlie the short distance and knocked on the back door where Millie was often working.

"Hello, girls. I just took cranberry almond pecan bread out of the oven."

"Yum," Emma said, taking off both of their coats.

While eating the cake, Emma asked, "You know the woman who came down for dinner my night here but didn't introduce herself? I wonder if she would like to come to Thanksgiving dinner. But, unfortunately, she is the only one who isn't coming."

"I am not sure she has somewhere to go. She is a pretty private person. She usually goes out in the morning but has not shared where she is going. Usually, she is back in time for tea here, which I include in the room's price. Not all of them enjoy tea as I do. Sometimes, she doesn't even come down for dinner. I don't intrude on my boarders' private lives."

"I understand that. Is Olive here right now?" Emma asked.

"Let me look up the stairs. We are cleaning the rooms today, so Olive's door will be open."

Just as Millie peeked up the stairs, the woman came down. "Good morning, Olive."

"Hello, Millie," she said, putting on her coat.

"Before you leave, come into the kitchen and meet Emma. She is house-sitting Michael's house while he is gone. Olive, this is Emma Morrison, Emma, this is Olive Coleman. Emma has something to ask you."

"Glad to meet you, Olive. I am having Thanksgiving dinner at Michael's house and wondered if you would like to come. I have asked some neighbors and the other boarders here. I would love to have you."

"That sounds nice. What time?" She looked rather pleased to be invited.

"We are gathering at 4:30 for drinks, and then we will eat around 5:00."

"Count me in. Thank you. See you both later," Olive said as she left the kitchen.

As soon as they heard the door close, Millie said, "She is a woman of few words. But she is very nice in her way. She's lived here for a long time, but we still know very little about her."

"I am so glad she said yes. I hate to think that anyone would spend the day alone."

"Thanks for thinking of her. That was thoughtful of you."

Around 3:00 pm, Emma packed up the chocolate chip cookies she had baked that afternoon and got Charlie ready to spend some time with Olivia while she went to the writing club.

After dropping off Charlie, she walked over to the bookstore. She and Elizabeth decided to put eleven chairs in a circle to talk and brainstorm ideas. They each had a few questions to get the conversation going. Introductions would be critical, especially to Ella Rose. Elizabeth had made some hot chocolate since the weather was colder.

A little after 3:30, teens started arriving, laughing, and talking with Ella Rose, who was right in the middle of the group.

"Hi, Ms. Morrison!" she said and hugged her. "Where is Charlie? I was going to show her off to the others."

"She's with Olivia for a couple of hours, depending on how long we talk and write."

As other middle school students arrived, they eagerly enjoyed the cookies and hot chocolate.

"Jonathan Reed will be late because he had to go to his dentist, but he will be here. Ms. Morrison, this is Jennifer Coggan."

Emma looked at Jennifer and loved her sweet smile. Emma was impressed that these teens were not so moody as she had seen other places.

"I met you at the B and B a week ago. You were so nice to bring a crib for Charlie," Emma said. "Nice to see you again."

"Please call me Jenn. I like working with Millie. She is so nice to me, and I can work around my schedule for school."

Elizabeth asked them to introduce themselves and tell one thing they wanted everyone to know about herself or himself as they sat down. Most of them seemed to be fond of reading and writing. Usually, they didn't like to be assigned stories to write, but they loved the club idea. Being in a club of any kind seemed to be an exception to that rule.

Elizabeth started the conversation and brainstorming for writing ideas by suggesting that they think of stories from childhood. It could be something funny or sad.

"I am thinking about the first time I ever babysat when I was about twelve," said Jenn, sitting next to Ella Rose. "The three boys were horrible, and they tried to play all kinds of pranks on me. Of course, I was upset at the time, but now that I think about it, it was funny."

"I was thinking of writing about the day I started school in Kansas City. Being new in a school can be intimidating, but one girl helped me with my locker combination," Ella Rose added.

Jonathan came in, smiling with his new braces. "What did I miss?" he asked.

They filled him in on the first two ideas the girls had shared. "I think I would like to write about getting my dog, Archie, a few years ago."

Elizabeth said she had an idea for a way to think of writing ideas. "Open your journals to the first page and draw a big circle or heart, write short memories, whatever you want. I will set a timer, and you write down everything you can remember, small or big. You will be the only person to see this paper. Write fast and think of your entire childhood. Ready, set, go. You have one minute."

Everyone there, including Elizabeth and Emma, wrote feverishly for the entire minute.

"Time," Elizabeth called. "That was a minute! How many ideas did you write down?"

"I can't believe I thought of so many things that happened to me," admitted Jonathan.

Some of the teens shared stories about grandparents, others about animals. Everyone wanted more time to write. They could sit anywhere around the bookstore and come back together in about a half-hour.

Both Elizabeth and Emma thought it would be helpful if they also wrote. Emma went over to the fireplace and sat down. She pondered what she could write about and still keep her secret. Maybe a childhood story about her and her sister would be okay. She stared at the flickering fire, and many fun memories with her sister came to mind. She started by writing down words to describe her sister, and the good memories brought a smile to her face. Emma thought maybe she could share the stories with Charlie when she got older. The half-hour went by so quickly.

Several teens had written about problems, but many wrote about funny situations. Jenn wrote about harmless pranks or tricks they had played on friends. Emma thought they were enjoying coming up with stories on their own.

"Emma and I thought we could have more sharing next week. Would that work for you all?" Elizabeth asked.

"What about coming every Monday for a month to discuss your stories?"

"What about coming in the day after Thanksgiving? We are out of school, and I don't want to go Christmas shopping with my mother and my aunts," said Jonathan, rolling his eyes.

"That would be fun," added Jenn, "Could we do that?"

"Emma, would that work for you?" Elizabeth asked. "I could stay after my storytime for toddlers if that works for you."

"I will check with either Millie and Olivia to see if they could watch Charlie."

"We could put her on a blanket in the middle of our circle," suggested Ella Rose, and everyone laughed, thinking of an almost toddler at their writing club.

The conversation lasted for another few minutes. It seemed to both Emma and Elizabeth that the teens enjoyed just talking, and writing had fueled some thoughts to share.

"Do you think we should have a title for our writing club?" Emma asked.

"That's a good idea," said Jonathan.

Emma shared, "Did you all know that Elizabeth's middle name is Paige?"

The kids looked confused for a few seconds, and then a few started laughing.

"Oh, that's how she thought of the name of the bookstore—The Paige Turner. So clever!" said Ella Rose.

"So, we could just call ourselves Paige's Pencil Pushers since some of us are using pencils to write," suggested Jenn.

They all laughed but agreed it would be a fun name, even though some would instead type on laptops. They decided they would share parts of their stories on Friday but decided to meet earlier in the day.

As Emma left the bookstore, she felt happy. She walked with Ella Rose until she turned off to pick up Charlie at Olivia's. She enjoyed writing childhood stories, but memories of her sister's illness and death were too sad. Nevertheless, it felt good to think of their happy childhood.

The following two days would be busy getting ready for Thanksgiving. She remembered that her dad always ordered pizza the night before Thanksgiving because her mother was busy cooking and bringing food prepared for the next day. Emma chuckled to herself and decided she would order a pizza. It would be a treat even though Charlie couldn't eat it. She would make Charlie mac and cheese, which was a favorite of hers. Emma followed her mother's ways by getting some dishes out the day before and organizing the kitchen. Finally, she went to bed feeling very productive and happy.

A few hours later, Emma sat up suddenly from a sound sleep. She was sweating, and her heart was pounding wildly. It was still dark, and the streetlights shined through the window curtains. She put her hand to her forehead and started to remember that she had had a dream about the day before she had left her home. Her memories of that terrible day continued to haunt her. Would she ever forget the scare, which led her to leave at midnight, not knowing where she was going? She drank some water from the glass she had left by her bed and laid down.

She tried to sleep by thinking about the beautiful day ahead with her new friends. It took a while, but she finally drifted off.

CHapter eleven

...in which Thanksgiving Day brings more surprises

Turkey Day

T hanksgiving morning began like in the movies with frost on the lawn and the pumpkins on the street's porches. The air was crisp, and the sky was as blue as blue can be in November. Emma shivered as she peeked out the front door to gaze at the sight. She vaguely remembered waking up during the night with bad memories, but today she was determined to enjoy her life now. She loved having time to savor quiet moments.

It made her remember seeing the play "Our Town" by Thornton Wilder years ago. The story made her cry but had a great lesson to appreciate the simple things in life. She had a small role in the play once in high school as a lady in the crowd. She marveled, especially at the monologue by Emily after her death, talking to those who had already died. She spoke of the wonder of life and how most of us ignore the seemingly small moments in our own lives.

Sipping her cup of coffee, Emma planned when to put the turkey in the oven. It would take about four hours. If they ate at 5:00 pm, she should probably put it in around 11:00 am. The Better Homes and Gardens Cookbook lay open on the counter, listing all the stuffing ingredients.

She thought of making waffles that morning, just like her mother used to do. The memory was a good one, not so sad anymore. She had found a great waffle maker in the pantry. It always surprised her to see things in the house of a bachelor. Who would think a man would ever make waffles for himself? She wanted to ask Olivia more about Michael. It was curious that she rarely mentioned him. Just then, Emma heard a cry from upstairs. Charlie was about to wake up.

She peeked around the doorframe and said, "Boo! Good morning, Peanut. Because today is Thanksgiving, I bought you a special outfit. Also, we are having guests for a fun dinner."

Charlie giggled as if she understood what Emma said. She raised her arms to get out of the crib and babbled a few words; one sounded like 'out.' Emma decided to dress her in play clothes for the morning and her nap. They would clean up after that.

Waffles and bacon were first on the schedule. Charlie pounded on the highchair's tray while Emma flipped the gourmet waffle maker and turned the bacon. She gave her Cheerios to tide her over until the waffles baked. Moments later, the phone rang as Emma cleaned up the syrup from Charlie's face. "I also feel sticky all over, but wasn't that yummy?" She asked Charlie questions, not expecting any answers.

"Hello, Olivia," Emma said, answering the phone. "I saw the caller ID. Happy Thanksgiving!"

"Same to you, Emma. We are looking forward to this afternoon. I can already imagine I smell the turkey. I might come over a little early if you don't mind. Millie will be over after that."

"That would be great. The Dolans and John will be over at about 4:30 pm, and I thought we could eat around 5:00 pm. Pat and Dave are bringing their granddaughter, also. So that should be fun."

"I hope so. I heard Pat talking about her not long ago. She was having a hard time in middle school and not making friends easily. Her middle school is huge in KC. I heard she has a chance to go to Truman Middle School while she is here. So maybe playing a little with Charlie will help her feel better."

"I hope so. Middle school can be a tough time for both boys and girls." She said that before, she thought Olivia might ask her about her earlier life. But unfortunately, she wasn't prepared to share anything yet.

Changing the subject, Emma said, "I might need a little advice about carving the turkey. My dad used to do it."

"I think I know how, but you mentioned that John might volunteer," Olivia added.

Emma laughed and agreed it would be good if he would take care of the carving. "So glad that Esther Grace, Mary Margaret, John, and Walter, could also come on! It will be a full house, for sure. I'm glad I also asked Olive Coleman. We had not talked the first day at the boarding house." Emma could not make up her mind about what to call Millie's home.

"They were all thrilled to have somewhere to go. It also gave Millie and me a break from cooking"

"See you soon."

The morning passed as Charlie entertained herself in her little playpen Millie had borrowed from an old friend. Emma made the stuffing and got the turkey ready for the oven. Emma watched Charlie throw her toys out of the playpen and then expect Emma to throw them back.

Charlie went down for a nap around two, which gave Emma a chance to make a centerpiece of the flowers she bought the day before and get out the candles. She had found brass candlesticks in the pantry. The butcher had sent the fresh turkey and stuffing ingredients over the day before just as he had offered. He even included a pound of butter in case Emma forgot to purchase any, which she had. Emma also paid the delivery person for the butter even though the butcher said she could bring the money in after Thanksgiving.

The extra extensions for the table made it very long, and it would comfortably seat twelve. Emma added Olive, but there would be plenty of room for her. Although she wondered about Michael's beautiful things, Emma did not have the nerve to ask Olivia anything about him.

The tablecloth fit perfectly! Since she didn't find cloth napkins, she put out a pretty paper one at each place setting. She stood back to admire the table and was delighted.

Emma changed her clothes, putting on a colorful sweater she found at The Unique Boutique downtown. She combed her hair before Charlie woke up from her nap. Finally, Emma dressed Charlie in an adorable shirt with a turkey on the front and her orange striped leggings. She looked sweet, Emma thought.

They were ready for their guests around 4:00 pm when the doorbell rang. Olivia was true to her word being early. It would be pleasant to talk while getting the wine and appetizers ready. Then, they could stand around in the kitchen to have drinks and a little something to eat before dinner. Emma was having so much fun that Olivia commented how happy she seemed as she came inside.

Emma gave her a big hug and said, "I had the best day getting ready for this meal. I have enjoyed taking care of this house. I so appreciate your trusting me to do it."

"Well, Emma, this house has never looked as good as it does now. Of course, Michael isn't here, but he doesn't seem to enjoy it that much, even here. But now, everything sparkles and shines. You have taken great care of the place."

"I can't help but be curious about him. I keep finding things I wouldn't think a bachelor would have," she said, remembering the waffle iron.

"Well, he was engaged a while back, but the young lady called it off when she learned he would be possibly gone for a year with his work. I think she left town and moved to St. Louis for a new job. She was in journalism also. Can't say I miss her."

Emma didn't even ask her name.

The discussion ended as the doorbell rang, and Millie came in with her dishes. She leaned over to kiss Emma on the cheek. "The turkey smells and looks wonderful. Hello, Charlie, I have a little present for you. I brought you a little stuffed turkey doll. It matches your sweater!"

Charlie hugged the toy turkey and started crawling toward the kitchen, dragging her new toy. The women all laughed. Emma felt a pleasant sensation of being part of a group, maybe like a family again. It made her think of her mother and father and what they might be doing right now. Finally, someone asked her where to put a dish, and she returned to the present.

The women became busy with dishes as Charlie watched them, chewing on her new doll. The doorbell rang. Mr. and Mrs. Dolan came in, bearing food and hostess gifts, followed by Ella Rose, who had her long strawberry blond hair fixed in a French braid. She looked like her grandmother and seemed happy to Emma. "Hello, Mr. and Mrs. Dolan. I am glad to see you again, Ella Rose. I love your name."

"Please call us Pat and Dave," said Mr. Dolan. "Makes us feel younger."

Ella Rose smiled at Emma. She peeked around the chair to look for the baby she had heard about from her grandmother. Charlie was so delighted with all the attention that she giggled and tried to stand up by a chair.

John came right after the Dolans with a box of chocolates for Emma and a little soft football for Charlie. The sisters, dressed in patchwork skirts and peasant blouses, were right after them. They looked so sweet. Emma couldn't help but respect them for wearing what they wanted and doing what they loved. They brought green beans with almond sauce for dinner and a colorful pull toy for Charlie. Olive came right behind the sisters; Emma guessed they had walked over together from the B and B.

"I forgot to ask you both," Emma said to the sisters, "How did the flowers go over on Saturday? We had such a good time making them."

Esther Marie answered with a thumbs-up. "They were very appreciative. Most of them have part-time jobs, and some save money for college. We had fun helping them."

Everyone stood around the kitchen, sharing cheese and crackers while waiting for Walter and Monroe. Emma thanked Millie for bringing the potatoes ready to be mashed. She got the turkey out of the oven to rest before carving. Emma had read the cookbook chapter on turkey twice to be sure to do it right. She still couldn't believe a bachelor would have a cookbook. She guessed it was an engagement gift.

Walter and Monroe came in last and brought more wine and some mixed nuts. They looked very dapper, Walter in a red blazer and a gold tie and Monroe in a festive plaid sport coat and white shirt. Emma wondered how old they were. She guessed that Millie would have made a Thanksgiving dinner at the B and B if she hadn't decided to host the meal. The candles glow from the table, and the subtle lighting in the dining room is warm and inviting.

The table looked beautiful, and Emma beamed at the compliments. She had enjoyed decorating it with pumpkins, gourds, and some autumn flowers. Music from the old stereo made an excellent background to the conversation around the table. When everyone sat down, and Charlie sat in her highchair, Emma stood up at the head to give a toast. "I am happy you are all here today. I feel grateful for your friendship," she said.

John said grace, followed by a moment of silence in the room. He carved the turkey as he had done in his own home through the years, and Emma was glad. John was an expert and passed the plates. Olivia started showing the other excellent dishes with appreciative sighs and enjoyment. Sitting next to John, Emma saw him sneak little bits of turkey to Charlie. She always gave her small pieces of food that she thought would be easy to eat with her fingers. Unfortunately, utensils were a bit complex for her. Ella Rose sat between her grandparents but couldn't keep her eyes off Charlie. She seemed fascinated with her playfulness as she tried to put food on her spoon. Walter and Monroe talked to Esther Marie and Mary Margaret, who loved the attention as much as Charlie did.

Seeing that Olive wasn't talking to anyone, she asked, "Olive, where did you grow up? Have you lived in Hill Brook all your life?"

Olive looked startled but answered, "No, my family traveled all around as my dad was in the Army. He was a Lt. Colonel in the United States Army. So we lived all over the world. When I married, we moved to Kansas City. After my husband died, I decided I needed a small town like Hill Brook. I love living at Millie's house."

"I bet you have a lot of stories to tell about your travels. Do you ever write down your memories?"

"I do remember all the different schools I attended. I went to three elementary schools, two middle schools, and two high schools. My dad relocated every few years."

Ella Rose looked up, shocked, and said, "That is amazing. I thought two schools were too many. I bet you have some amazing stories from around the world. Would you be willing to come to our writing club on Friday? We would love to hear your stories."

"Are you sure teenagers would be interested in my stories!" Olive asked.

"I am," said Ella Rose, and Olive smiled at her.

Emma asked Ella Rose what classes she was taking her first semester at Truman. Eighth grade was a great year as the move to high school could be a challenge.

"I was able to join the Algebra and French classes here as electives. I like French and look forward to going to Paris someday."

"It is so exciting to have experiences like travel. Did your school in Kansas City sponsor a trip to Europe?" Emma asked her.

"I think next year, if we stay in Kansas City, I might have the chance to sign up for the trip. That would make high school more interesting to me."

"What do you mean if you stay in Kansas City?" Olivia asked her.

"Well, Mom and Dad can do their export business anywhere. I will try to get them to move here. I feel like a small-town girl."

Her grandmother leaned over and hugged her, "Well, we would love you to stay." Her grandfather patted her shoulder, and Emma thought he had tears in his eyes.

"That would be great to have you all here in Hill Brook," he added, sniffling a little.

Changing the subject, Emma asked Ella Rose, "Did you like the first writing club meeting?"

"It was great. I can't wait to talk about what each of us writes tomorrow," Ella Rose told them the name of the writing club - Paige's Pencil Pushers. They all laughed.

"What are you all writing about?" asked Mary Margaret.

"Emma remembered writing in school. She thought maybe we could have a writing club where we write whatever we want, not just for an assigned topic. Emma, I peeked at your brainstorming paper, and you had a large "Q" on it. What does that mean?"

"When I was growing up, my mother had a wooden "Q" on her kitchen wall. She always told us that if we made it to "Q," we were living well in the alphabet of life."

Everyone nodded, agreeing with the sentiment.

Ella Rose turned to Mary Margaret and said, "Emma got the idea of writing stories, which led us to wonder how Mr. Evans got involved with whirligigs." She turned to John and asked him if he could come. "Emma thinks everyone has stories. That made her think of having a writing club. I loved the brainstorming we did Monday. We decided to meet tomorrow to continue the discussion."

John laughed and said, "I might have to come to your writing club and write about whirligigs. I would be glad to tell you why I got into whirligigs. Then, I could maybe write my story down."

"It is a great idea to write down things that happen to us. Memories are important. Some of them bought journals, but some used their laptops.

Elizabeth Turner and I hoped that Ella Rose and her new friends might like it," admitted Emma.

"Good luck with your writing and possible travels to Paris!" Walter and Monroe said, almost in unison. "We buy popcorn from the kids at the high school here for their fundraiser. I bet your high school back home will do the same."

Ella Rose nodded and smiled, and Emma thought she was pleased with the attention paid to her.

"Emma, we are happy you stayed in Hill Brook. I feel as if Michael's home sparkles from top to bottom. I was hoping I would hear from him, but phone lines in the Middle East are unreliable," said Olivia.

"I love this house, and Charlie loves it, too! The kitchen is wonderful. I guess Michael remodeled it at some point."

"He hired a contractor after he bought it, which was before his wedding."

Emma nodded, thinking of the sadness he must have felt when his fiancée canceled the engagement. She wondered if that was one reason he left to go somewhere in the Middle East.

John caught Emma's eye, winked quickly, and turned to Monroe and Walter. He asked if they had some spare time before Christmas. Before dinner, Emma had suggested that maybe Walter and Monroe would like to be included in making the whirligigs that he was preparing for the Christmas festival.

"I certainly have some spare time, but I have to fit it around my morning and afternoon walks through town," Monroe said, smiling at Walter, who loved their walks.

"What do you have in mind, John?" asked Walter.

"Well, I make whirligigs in my basement to sell at the festival. I also make them all year round for Harley's Hill Brook Hardware."

Emma laughed," The people in this town love funny names for their businesses, don't they? "

"Well," John added, "Harley loves alliteration, for sure."

Everyone at the table laughed at that thought.

"Well, what do you say, guys? Could you help me out? I would recommend old clothes because there is some sawdust when we cut the shapes and sand. I have lots of great patterns. I usually make a few Santa whirligigs this time of year."

Monroe looked at Walter, who nodded and said, "We would enjoy helping you. It will keep us out of Millie's hair and out of trouble."

Millie spoke up as she brought in the two pies that Pat Dolan had baked. "You guys could never cause trouble!" she said as she winked at Olivia. Both women had talked about how the two men needed something besides reading and taking lots of walks to occupy themselves.

Emma walked into the kitchen as she cleared the table. She paused at the kitchen sink and just listened to the conversation in the dining room. It was comforting to hear the voices of people she had just met. It helped not miss her parents so much. It was a wonderful evening.

CHaPTer TWeLVe

...in which Emma's Goose is cooked

As Millie served the pies, everyone started sharing fond memories of past Thanksgiving. No one seemed to be sad about it, but more of a pleasant feeling of days past. They started laughing when someone remembered the movie, "A Christmas Story," about a family on Christmas when the neighbor's dogs came in and stole their turkey. The family ended up ordering roasted duck with its head still on in a Chinese restaurant. They all laughed at the memory of the movie.

As everyone lingered over coffee, Emma noticed Charlie was getting sleepy.

"I will put her down, and we can still visit for a little while. But, then, I will be right back," she said as she lifted Charlie out of the highchair.

No one was in a hurry to go home. Charlie had to throw kisses at everyone and hugged both Olivia and Millie. She finally put her head down on Emma's shoulder as they started up the stairs. After Emma was out of hearing, John asked how long Emma would stay in Hill Brook. "I hope she will stay for the whole year Michael is gone. Taking care of the house was too hard for me. One house per person is plenty," said Olivia with a sigh.

Ella Rose said, "I would be glad to babysit for Charlie anytime while I am in Hill Brook."

Olivia smiled at her, "That would be nice, and give Emma a break now and then. Raising a child can be exhausting for sure."

A pleasant lull in the conversation spread over the dining room as they sipped their coffee until they all heard a door key rattling in the front door.

"Who could that be?" asked Millie.

All those at the dining room table looked shocked as a large young man with a cowboy hat on his head entered the room with a satchel over one shoulder. His hair was shaggy. It was longer than Olivia had ever seen it. His clothes were rumpled, and she had never seen him look so angry.

He looked startled to see everyone. "What the heck is going on?"

"Michael!" Olivia shouted, rising from her seat. "Son, what are you doing back so soon?"

"It's a long story. I am going to bed. You can let yourselves out."

"Michael. Don't be rude. We are guests of your housekeeper."

"What are you saying? I don't have a housekeeper."

"Yes, you do. You left me in charge, and I couldn't take care of two houses at my age. I am not a spring chicken, you know." Her hands were on her hips, and she was shocked and puzzled by his looks and attitude.

Taken aback by her words, he said, "Well, fire her. I am back, and I don't need a housekeeper."

Olivia looked at her son, astonished by his appearance. His face was sunburned, and his hair was over his neck. He almost looked dirty, which was not his usual appearance. Moreover, he seemed angry, upset, and very tired. She was determined, however, to stand up for Emma.

"That's not going to happen, son. I gave her a year contract." She cringed, knowing she had done no such thing. There was no way she would kick out that girl and baby who needed some help.

Michael dropped his duffle bag and sighed. Emma came down the stairs just about that time, not realizing the scene below. "Well, someone is asleep fast tonight." She looked at those at the dining table and turned to look where they were staring. The man in front of her was handsome but rough, with several days of a beard. She had the feeling she had seen him somewhere before. The memory was vague.

"You must be the housekeeper," he said with a snarl.

"And who are you?" she asked, almost afraid of the answer.

"I am your employer, I guess," Michael said, looking at his mother with a questioning look. "Look, I will help you find another place and job, but I need to be alone." Emma's face paled when he said that, and she put her hand on a chair nearby to steady herself.

He turned and walked up the stairs, leaving all the dinner guests, especially Emma, Olivia, and Millie, totally speechless.

Olivia thought Emma would burst into tears, but she said, "Guess I should start packing after we clean up dinner dishes." She held on to the chair as she was afraid to let go. She had never felt so shocked. There were tears in her eyes.

"Nonsense," Olivia said, "We will work something out. I promised you a year of employment and a place to live. I don't go back on my word. We will talk to Michael in the morning. Let's clean up. I bet there are lots of leftovers for the next few days."

John looked over at Olivia, and he winked at her as she smiled back. Emma wasn't sure what to make of that. Then Mary Margaret, Esther Marie, Walter, and Monroe excused themselves right away, looking embarrassed. They wondered what would happen next.

Olive whispered to Ella Rose, "I just might come to Paige's Pencil Pushers. Are you sure you wouldn't mind?"

"Not at all. Please come," Ella Rose answered.

If either Olivia or Millie was worried, they didn't show it. Emma was impressed that Michael's words hadn't seemed to affect them. Pat hugged her before they started clearing the dishes, and Dave and Ella Rose left after helping carry plates to the kitchen. Emma blew out the candles and felt a little light had gone out of her life. Having this house had been too good to be true. She had known it wouldn't last forever, but now she could be in trouble. She had never signed anything formal with Olivia.

CHapter THIrTeen

...in which John saves the day

There was an awkward silence while Olivia, Millie, John, and the Dolans helped clean up the dishes, wrapped left-overs, and tidied the dining room. Then, finally, Michael went to his room and threw his backpack in the corner. He wasn't as furious as he had been a few minutes before. Instead, Michael felt ashamed of his reaction to the people at the dinner table. He only noticed his mother and John but no one else at the table.

He knew he had shocked his mother and scared the young woman who came down the stairs. She seemed startled by his presence. When he said she had to leave, he noticed tears in her eyes.

Michael went into the bathroom and looked in the mirror; he saw a stranger. He was shocked to see his hair so shaggy, and it was apparent he had not looked in a mirror for weeks? Several questions came to mind! One, would he ever recover?

He lay down on the bed, barely pulling up the bedspread before hitting the pillow. A fragrance of the summer breeze overwhelmed him as he drifted off to sleep.

Downstairs, no one said much until Olivia came over to Emma and gave her shoulders a big hug. She said, "Don't worry, we will work this out. Michael looks a little worn down. Something must have happened on assignment for him to come home so soon. I am a little worried about him."

Emma added, "He did seem upset, especially finding us here." Although she hadn't gotten a good look at him, Emma thought he had been the restaurant person the first night she was in Hill Brook. "I can leave in the morning after I check the train schedules."

"Oh, no," Millie said, "Don't do anything rash. I think Olivia might be able to work it out."

After they all left, the house seemed quiet and unfriendly with the grumpy man upstairs. How could she and Charlie live a day with that man? She turned on the dishwasher and tidied the kitchen until she heard the water swishing in the machine. Emma turned out all the lights and made sure to lock the doors. She quietly headed upstairs and peeked into Charlie's room. She heard a soft breathing sound from the crib. She prayed Charlie would not wake up crying loudly.

Emma sat down on the bed. Her head was spinning with the problems that faced her. How could she stay in a single man's home, especially with some issue? Eventually, she changed into her nightgown, brushed her hair, and lay down. She didn't think she would ever get to sleep but would try, as the next day might prove to be very difficult. She would miss her new friends, especially Olivia and Millie, who had been kind.

After a late evening tossing and turning about what she and Charlie would do next, Emma slept until 9 am. Charlie also slept late after such an exciting and busy Thanksgiving Day. The day after was always a little less appealing, and today was doubly so. As the pale morning sun came through her bedroom window, Emma woke slowly and stretched. Then she remembered what had happened the night before. Emma looked at the clock and realized both had slept because of those events. She quickly dressed pulled her hair back into a ponytail, with her curls escaping everywhere. As she opened the door to check on a sleeping Charlie, she could hear voices coming from the kitchen.

She eased down the stairs, straining to hear who was speaking. As she turned the corner into the kitchen, she saw Olivia sitting with Michael, drinking coffee. "Good morning, Emma," greeted Olivia as she looked over Michael's shoulder. He didn't turn around, just stared into his cup of coffee. "Did you sleep okay?" she asked.

Emma shyly said, "I have never slept so late! Must have been tired from the Thanksgiving festivities."

Olivia reached for a piece of paper sitting by her chair and asked, "Would you like some coffee?"

Emma went over to the coffee maker without answering, pouring herself a cup. She sat down across the table from Michael, avoiding looking at him. She quietly sipped the coffee, not saying anything but dreading what was coming.

"Michael and I have been discussing the situation, and I showed him the contract we wrote several weeks ago."

Emma's head snapped up when Olivia said this. She tried not to look shocked at the paper Olivia held in her hands. She knew there was no contract other than a verbal commitment on both of their parts. She drew in a deep breath and said, "And what is the decision?" Anticipating the answer, she looked back into her coffee cup.

"We both feel the contract is firm, and you need to stay in the job if you are willing," Olivia said as she handed the contract to Emma.

She looked over the contract and was shocked to see a signature that looked just like her handwriting. She had to admit it looked professional, and it gave her some courage. Then, taking a deep breath, she looked directly at Michael, who was now looking at her. She knew she looked a little unkempt but held her head high. "Is this okay with you, Michael?" He looked as if he had not had much sleep the night before.

"I don't have much choice! A contract is a contract, and I trust my mother's judgment."

Emma felt some relief, although his attitude didn't make her feel very welcome. He didn't even know about Charlie yet. She was sure Olivia had not mentioned her. Just as that thought went through her mind, Charlie started crying from upstairs.

"What the hell is that noise?" Michael asked as his head looked up toward the stairs.

"That's Charlie!" Olivia answered.

"Who is that?" he asked.

"She is the cutest baby girl you would ever hope to meet," Olivia said with a smile. "Let me go get her. Would you mind starting breakfast, Emma?" Olivia was hoping to give her something to do.

"I think I will make pancakes," responded Emma, walking to the kitchen cabinet.

Silence filled the kitchen as Emma mixed up a batter for Charlie's favorite pancakes. Emma had her back turned toward Michael, and she ignored him while she warmed up the skillet and poured milk into Charlie's cup.

"Look who is wide awake," Olivia said as she carried Charlie into the kitchen. Michael looked up briefly and then looked down into his cold coffee. Charlie spotted him right away and turned her face into Olivia's shoulder. She peeked a bit as she sat in her highchair. Then, she grabbed her spill proof cup and looked toward Emma as if she needed reassurance about being here with the stranger in the room.

Charlie started babbling her baby talk as she played with Emma's spoon. "Is that so?" Emma asked her. "I agree with everything you said," she added, ruffling Charlie's hair and smiling.

Michael just kept staring at his coffee cup and didn't lookup.

Emma kept busy fixing the pancakes and offered both Olivia and Michael some. Olivia took some with a smile on her face, but Michael shook his head, which Emma ignored. When she put four on a plate and placed it in front of him, he grunted. Emma turned her back but couldn't help smiling. She gave a cut-up pancake to Charlie and a couple to herself before she sat down across from Michael. She was almost daring him to eat them. He finally picked up the syrup, cut up the pancakes, chewed them, said a quiet, "Thanks." Then, he left the kitchen to go upstairs.

"Oh, that went well," Olivia whispered to Emma with a smile.

Emma whispered back, "How did you come up with a contract as fast as you did, and who forged my signature?" she asked, looking at the professional-looking document that Olivia had shown Michael.

"Millie and I went to John's home last night. He is quite the wizard on the computer, so he designed it and printed it out. Millie got her registry from her B and B and forged your signature pretty well if I say so myself."

"You three are the best, but I hate to deceive Michael," Emma said quietly.

Olivia winked and said, "It is for his good. I am not sure what happened on his assignment, but it must have been not good. He doesn't seem himself. Even when he was younger, he has never been a happy-go-lucky kind of person, but this is different. He almost seems depressed, although I am glad he ate your pancakes."

"Well, I will try to be quiet! Maybe all he needs is rest." They both looked over at Charlie, who had syrup everywhere, including in her hair. Then, they both started laughing, and everything seemed a little brighter to Emma.

At least Emma had the writing club to anticipate. As they put on coats and Emma wrapped Charlie with an extra blanket, she remembered the writing club. It was too late to take Charlie to Olivia or Millie. The teens might enjoy Charlie sitting in the middle of the circle, as she hoped they might.

Emma got to the bookstore just as the teens were coming down the street. Ella Rose ran over to see and kiss Charlie. "You came. I am so glad. I missed you."

"I lost track of time, and it was too late to ask Olivia."

"No problem. We like babies," said Jenn.

Seeing Elizabeth setting up the chairs, Emma said, "I am so sorry I am late. Things are a little unsettled today."

"Did you have a good Thanksgiving?"

"It's a long story."

"Maybe we can talk after the writing club."

"Sure, we can stay a little bit."

The group gathered around, and Emma decided to put Charlie on a blanket in the middle of the group, as Ella Rose suggested.

"Do you want to continue the discussion about your brainstorming and then break to write?"

"Let's share a couple of ideas each and then start our writing. I like to hear other people's ideas," said Jenn.

Just as they were about to start sharing, Olive came in the door and shyly looked down but asked, "Am I too late?"

Ella Rose jumped up and got another chair to make room for her. "Come sit by me."

"Everyone, this is Olive Coleman. I think she has lots of stories to share," Emma said.

Looking around at the others, she was delighted they seemed to let a person from an older generation join a group their ages. She had always tried to include people of all ages in conversations.

They all waved at her, and she smiled back. Emma explained what they were about to do, and they started going around the circle as they shared ideas. Each idea led to others thinking about that idea. For example, one person thought he would write about a childhood dog, which reminded others of a dog story. They spent about ten minutes sharing ideas.

Elizabeth then set her iPhone alarm to thirty minutes and reminded them they could sit anywhere. Luckily, she had beanbag chairs around the room. Emma went back to the fireplace for this session. She sat Charlie on her lap while she wrote in her journal on the arm of the chair.

Emma was thrilled that the discussions allowed them to share their memories. Her childhood memories were happy ones, and writing them down might help her get over what happened recently. For some reason, memories of her sister kept returning. It must have been helpful to remember her childhood after the past few painful months. So it was essential to writing down stories for Charlie to hear as she grew up.

She wrote about the fort they made in the woods behind their house in elementary school. The neighborhood kids would rush to meet after school to work on it. It became a secret among them. They had found a hole back in the woods and decided it would be a magnificent underground fort. They would dig it out, make it bigger, and cover it with logs and leaves. Emma wrote as much as she could remember, especially about Susie looking to find the wood to go on top. The branches had to be a specific size to fit. The group spent weeks on it.

When the alarm on Elizabeth's phone sounded, she was startled at how quickly the time had passed. Charlie was sitting on the floor by Emma's feet, playing with Elizabeth's wooden toy in the reading corner. After they sat back down in their circle, the group decided that they would like some writing time at the next gathering to finish their stories before sharing. Elizabeth said part of the writing process would be to edit each other's writing.

During that part of the discussion, Charlie decided to start crawling from one teen to another. Ella Rose picked her up for a bit, but Jenn said, "We have been talking for an hour." So they agreed to meet the following Monday again to discuss their stories.

After the group left, Emma shared briefly with Elizabeth that Michael had returned for some unknown reason, but he had not shared what had happened.

Elizabeth said, "You know I went to school with Michael. When I was a freshman, he was a senior and was always a nice guy. Maybe time and quiet will help. I bet he will come around. Does it seem physical, or do you think it is emotional?"

"I don't think it is physical, but I haven't talked to him much. He is letting me stay, though. I am trying to be quiet so he can rest. Thanks again for the writing club. I think the kids are getting a lot from the conversations."

Olive was listening and waiting so she could walk back with Emma. She nodded at what she heard from their conversation.

"I love it, and I sold some journals," Elizabeth added. "I am encouraging some of the older folks in town to get involved in a writing group. They can meet here and maybe buy a few books. Their generation needs to write down their memories also. Many of them are researching family history and writing stories about their ancestors. Thanks for thinking of the idea of writing for the teen group. You never know who will purchase a book or paper supplies. I tried to improve the store when I first came. I hired Joe Hampton to design the store's layout and build a counter for check out. He did a great job."

"I thought Joe was a handyman. I didn't know he was a builder."

"Oh, he is more than that. He trained as an architect, worked in Chicago for a while, and came back to work here. I think he hated city life."

"Good to know more about him," Emma said, shaking her head.

"See you next Monday," Emma said as she and Olive left The Paige Turner, chuckling over the apt name.

"Thanks for coming to the writing club, Olive. I am sure your stories will be so interesting. Do you smell snow in the air?"

"I do," she said, looking toward the overcast sky, "I will listen to the weather forecast when we get back," Olive said.

Emma wasn't worried about that possibility, as there was plenty of food in the pantry and the freezer was as packed as it was when she started this job. Then, she remembered that the girl at Molly's had mentioned electricity problems sometimes with storms. "I will need to look for candles and flashlights, just in case," she said to Olive, who agreed.

Emma waved goodbye to Olive when they got to Millie's, and Emma continued home.

Chapter Fourteen

...in which Emma walks on eggshells

On the Saturday after Thanksgiving, Emma decided to take Charlie out to stroll around the neighborhood. The weather was reasonably mild, and the sun was bright. Some leaves had fallen, and the colors weren't as beautiful. Nevertheless, the air smelled clean and fresh. It seemed a wise idea to leave the house quiet for Michael, who had gone upstairs and closed his door. Maybe he just needed sleep, and he would feel better. It would be awkward no matter what had happened to him, but Emma thought she had little choice but to leave the house for a walk.

She put Charlie in her new hat and coat. It had been great to have some money to spend on Charlie. Unfortunately, her original stash was almost gone, and she needed her salary from Olivia. She looked back on the past month and realized she had not quite thought through escaping a bad situation. At the time, there was no choice but to take Charlie and leave as quickly as possible. Thoughts of those times came back to her. She shook her head to banish them. She looked down at Charlie, sitting so excitedly in her stroller. "Are you ready to go?" Emma asked.

Charlie bounced up and down. Odd they went down the street toward town. She knew she would pass the Hyacinth Bed and Breakfast and the café with the funny name, where she had eaten the first night. She didn't intend to go into either, but her question about Michael continued to bother her. Why would Michael have come to town and then not gone home?

Where had he stayed, and why didn't anyone recognize him? She had so many questions and no answers. Emma didn't feel she could mention it to Olivia. It would have worried her more than she already was. She had become very dear to Emma in the past few weeks.

She waved at Millie, who was sweeping the front porch of the B and B. "Hello, Emma and Charlie, how is everything this morning?" Emma didn't feel like saying anything negative about the situation, but she knew Millie had been in on the contract hoax. "Okay! We are shopping at the market."

Emma passed the café without stopping and headed into Molly's Market. What a quaint name, she thought to herself. With so many leftovers in the refrigerator from Thanksgiving, they didn't need groceries. Suddenly, she remembered a meal her mother had made on the day after Thanksgiving. The dish was called Turkey a la King and was delicious using leftover turkey and adding peas, carrots, and mushrooms. She decided to pick up the extra ingredients to make the dish. It was a sweet memory, and Emma wished to call her mom to get the exact recipe. After that, she would improvise as she went along.

"Hi, Little Missy," said a lady in the bakery. Charlotte must be off work. "Hi, Mom, could she have a cookie? The best part of my job is giving away cookies!"

"That would be nice," Emma answered.

"Here is your cookie, Little Miss."

Charlie grabbed the cookie after Emma took off her mittens. Charlie's face lit up as she munched on the cookie. Emma thought that so many people were friendly like this young woman; she would love to stay here.

"Thanks for her mid-morning snack. It is nice outside, considering the time of year."

"Well, it can change fast. We sometimes get some snow in mid-December. A couple of years ago, we had nearly two feet of snow. It was beautiful, but we lost power in some places. So we all hunkered down for a few days. It is nice to slow down, though, once in a while. By the way, I am Connie Welkins; we haven't met."

"I am Emma. I am house-sitting for a friend. My little friend in the stroller is Charlie. Thanks again! I will make Turkey a la King, which was a recipe from my mom. I think I can figure it out."

"Yum! That sounds perfect for the day after Thanksgiving. Have fun."

Emma went over to the vegetable counter and remembered there was celery in the recipe. Charlie happily munched on her cookie while Emma purchased all the makings.

On their way home, she passed by the café. She couldn't resist going in to see if the owner had noticed a man in a cowboy hat. She probably wouldn't remember, but it might be interesting to find something out about that mystery man.

"Hello," Emma said to the woman behind the counter. But, unfortunately, she was not Maggie Hoxie, who had been so friendly the night she arrived in town. Emma had been so exhausted and worried that night.

"Hello, you two. Welcome to the neighborhood. Glad to meet you. Where are you staying?"

"I am house sitting for Olivia Williams. Her son has been on overseas assignment for a cable network." She wasn't about, to tell the truth, that Michael was back. That wasn't something for her to share.

"Could I get you a cup of tea and milk for your little girl?" the waitress asked.

"Sure!" Emma said, wishing she had asked her name.

"I am Ellen Jordan," she said as if she had read Emma's mind.

When the waitress returned with their drinks, Emma asked if she had been working there for a long time.

"No, and I usually work part-time; the owner usually works the night shift. She seems to like that time of day. Do you want to talk to her?"

"Only if it is no trouble. Is the owner here?"

"Sure, she is in the kitchen making pies. I'll get her."

Emma waited a bit, and she smiled as the owner walked out, wiping her hands off. She had flour on her nose and a big smile on her face. "Oh, hi there, I heard you were helping out Olivia. She is delighted you decided to stay in town. I am Nelly Blanding. You may have met my son, Josh, the town police chief. You know he is single," she added with a wink.

"Hi! I met him and his partner recently." She was wary of asking too many questions, but she plowed ahead, "I wonder if you remembered a man with a cowboy hat here a couple of weeks ago?"

"Hum, not really, but then again, serving dinners at night with one waitress and just me can be rather hectic. Should I have noticed him?"

"Well, he was tall and looked a little seedy, and he kept his hat on and pulled down over his face. I thought you might have known him from being around."

"Well, not really. Then again, serving dinners at night with one waitress and just me can be rather hectic. Should I have noticed him? Sorry I can't help!"

"That's okay. I was just wondering. Thanks."

Emma went over to the counter to pay for the drinks. She had procrastinated long enough but had to go back to the house no matter the situation. After that, she could keep busy making dinner.

The house seemed quiet when she walked in. Charlie was acting sleepy, so Emma took her upstairs to nap. The door to Michael's room was closed, and she heard no noise. So when did she start to think of him as Michael?

She felt strained being in the house with someone so hostile, but she had to keep going. Millie, Olivia, and John had done much to keep her there. She was grateful but nervous.

Emma went through the dining room, remembering the joy of Thanksgiving dinner before Michael's return. She paused for a minute, enjoying the flowers still in the middle of the table. Then, as she turned toward the kitchen, Emma heard the water running. She saw Michael bending over the sink and not moving.

"Are you okay?" she asked, hoping he had heard her enter the house a while ago. She didn't want to startle him, especially since he didn't want her there at all.

At first, he didn't move or turn toward her. Then he turned his head and glanced over his shoulder, not touching the rest of his body. "Oh, I am just dandy!" he said sarcastically.

"Could I fix you lunch or something? You must be hungry after missing dinner last night and having had just a few pancakes this morning," she said as she walked into the kitchen. A little milky sunlight came through the window. It was not a happy moment for either one of them.

"I'm not hungry," he said perfectly still. Maybe he was going to throw up, Emma thought.

She jumped right into the mix with, "Well, I will make my mom's favorite day- after-Thanksgiving dinner meal, which is called Turkey a la King. I just went to Molly's to get the other things I needed. It was always a special leftover meal in my family!" She knew she was babbling but couldn't help herself. The words were just something to fill the emptiness of the room.

Michael slowly turned around and straightened up. Her employer was very tall and broad in the shoulders with long, dark brown hair and looked as if he hadn't had a haircut in a long time. Emma didn't think he had taken off his clothes to sleep the previous night.

He looked her up and down, making her feel a little jittery. There wasn't much to see. Emma was always aware of being short and a little plump. Those features were not what men appreciated in a woman. Her best feature was her hair, but today she twisted it into a careless ponytail. She wasn't wearing much makeup.

"No, I just need to sleep. Where is the little rugrat?" Michael asked, heading for the stairs.

Emma thought she heard a little humor in his voice, but maybe not. "You mean Charlie? Well, she, too, needs to nap during the day. Hopefully, she will be quiet while you sleep. I will keep her down here when she wakes up." Emma was trying to be as accommodating as she could be.

He turned without answering and headed for the stairs.

Emma exhaled in relief as he left, enjoying the more comfortable room now. She brushed her hair off her forehead as she put the vegetables on the butcher-block cutting board and took the leftover turkey out of the refrigerator. Then, starting to make dinner, Emma relaxed somewhat, thinking about the man who lived here for the undetermined future. Although, in some of the historical romance books she loved to read, living with a bachelor would ruin a girl's reputation forever for making a good marriage. Luckily, she was living in a different century.

Charlie woke about an hour later, and Emma fixed a snack. She was at that stage where she was hungry all the time. She bet there would be times she wouldn't want to eat, but this was fun watching her eat with enthusiasm.

"Slow down, missy, you are getting half in your mouth and a half on the floor," she said, laughing. A melancholy thought crossed her mind, wishing her sister could be there right now. That wasn't going to happen. Emma quickly returned to the stove. She stirred the butter and flour doe the roué and then thinned it out with a bit of milk. After many years of watching her mother make the recipe was easy to make.

After stirring the turkey and vegetables into the sauce, she put the dish into the refrigerator to be heated up later. The afternoon usually involved a walk around the neighborhood. Emma thought it would be wise for them to leave the house. Although she had rarely seen Michael, she felt his unfriendly presence all the time.

The weather was changing, but it felt good to be outside again. Emma walked around the block and ended up in front of Olivia's house, hoping she might be home. Emma knocked on the back door where Olivia usually did something in the kitchen or her little hearth room. Luckily, she was home and welcomed them both enthusiastically. She was very curious about how Michael was doing.

"Well, how does my son seem today?" she asked with a wink.

"He seems tired and sad about something," Emma answered. "I don't think he wants company right now, so we are trying to stay out of his way. I am glad he ate some pancakes this morning, though."

"I think that is a good sign! He was always a good eater as a teenager."

Olivia poured Emma a cup of tea on a saucer with a bit of cranberry scone tucked in and gave Charlie a cut-up banana. Emma looked at Olivia and said, "I always wished for a neighbor like you." She took a sip of the tea and a bite of the scone and said, "Yum!" She added, "I don't want to cause problems, but I think I saw Michael the night I arrived in Hill Brook. I can't be sure because he had a cowboy hat on his face. I never got a clear look at him. Why would he have been in town for a while without coming over to his house or your house?" she wondered aloud.

"That is strange. Michael hasn't always shared his problems with me. He and his dad had a great relationship and talked often. I was worried that he had no one to confide in, especially when his fiancée called off the wedding. That was a rough time."

"When did your husband die?" Emma asked reluctantly.

"About three years ago, but he had been ill for some time with heart issues. He tried to eat well and exercise, but it wasn't enough. He was the love of my life, and I miss him every day. I know Michael also does."

"I am so sorry for your loss. You seem to have lots of friends around, and everyone just loves you, like Charlie and me. Your kindness to a perfect stranger has been overwhelming to me," Emma said with tears forming.

"Thank you, Emma, but we are thrilled to meet you and Charlie," she said, putting her hand over Emma's. "Both Millie and I had an instinct you were sent here for a reason. I don't know why you came to town, but we felt you taking the housekeeper's job was perfect for all of us. No one wants to intrude on your privacy. We will give you time to talk to us when you feel like it. However, Michael returning has challenged us, but we will work it out."

"I still can't believe you and Millie got John to create that contract so fast!"

"Michael was speechless when I showed it to him. He was sure we had hired you on a handshake," Olivia said.

"Which was true," Emma replied. They both laughed at their little white lie. "Thank you for the afternoon treat! You must be the best baker around."

As they left the porch, Olivia noticed a few snowflakes flying around. "Oh dear, I just heard a prediction of snow. It is a little early because we usually don't get snow until later in December. I hope we don't get too much to ruin the holiday festivities. Christmas is just a few weeks ahead."

Bundling up, Emma and Charlie headed back to Michael's house. His presence had undoubtedly changed her feeling about being there. She had no choice but to soldier through the situation, especially for Charlie's sake. She wished she could confide in Olivia about her problems.

The house was quiet when Emma closed the door behind her. Charlie had fallen asleep on the way back from Olivia's home. The snow started to stick on the grass, but not on the concrete sidewalks. Maybe it wouldn't amount to much, she hoped.

Charlie curled up in her little playpen with her toys. Emma brushed back a curl off her forehead as she sighed, hugging her stuffed turkey. What a darling child, she thought. I will take care of her and protect her, no matter what happens.

She tiptoed downstairs, trying not to make noise. Staying in this house would be tough, trying to be quiet, not disturbing Michael. She assumed he was in his room as she thought he had been most of the day. She and Charlie ate turkey quietly that night and went to bed without Michael coming downstairs.

CHapTer FIFTeen

...in which a cold turkey leg helps Michael

On Monday, Emma went to the writing club's third meeting. She enjoyed the way the teenagers were digging down into their stories. Some wanted to type up their accounts to give to their families for Christmas. Emma brought up meeting John Evans and how he turned to make whirligigs after his wife died. The boys hoped to see how to assemble whirligigs, but the girls loved how they moved in the wind. Emma was sure there was a story behind his decision to make them, and she told the group she would ask him to come to one of the writing clubs.

As they made their way home, Emma thought about writing down so many stories. The rest of the week passed very slowly, with Emma trying to keep Charlie quiet. She guessed that Michael would come downstairs in the middle of the night and find something in the refrigerator because she rarely saw him during the day. Her best idea was to take a morning and an afternoon walk with Charlie so the house would be quiet for him. But, unfortunately, he might have gone out while she took her turns outside. She didn't know what else she could do to help him.

Later, Emma went over to the Dolans to let Charlie play with Ella Rose.

"Hi Ms. Morrison, come on in." Then, turning to Charlie in her arms, she said, "Hi Charlie," who smiled at her.

"How have you enjoyed the writing club?" Emma asked.

"It's great! It has been a way to make new friends at my school. My parents seem to be traveling more and more with their exporting business. I miss them, but I hate to miss even a few days of school. They called last night and told Grandma they were not returning for a while, maybe even after the holidays."

"I didn't realize they were into exporting. So you don't think your parents will be here for the holidays?" Emma asked.

"I don't think so," she answered sadly. "But I am so glad I enrolled here in Hill Brook. I like being at a smaller school. The writing club has helped me get to know some of the eighth-graders. I was never sure about the people at my school in Kansas City. Everyone seemed to be in a clique and group. I never fit in very well ever since we moved from Topeka last year."

"Your grandmother said that you would be willing to watch Charlie for me a few hours now and then."

"Sure, I would love that! Just let me know when."

"Mary Margaret and Esther Jane invited me to come to their church circle meeting and see what they are making for the holiday festival. I thought it might be fun to meet more people and maybe help them make something. I also heard about a Christmas Eve pageant at Hill Brook Community Church with all kinds of parts. Maybe you could join them while you are here. I bet rehearsals are fun."

"That's a good idea. I think that is the church that the Williams family attends and Millie. I might ask them."

Ella Rose shyly changed the conversation. "That was strange when Olivia's son came in on Thanksgiving night. I only met him last summer one time while I was visiting, and this time he looked like a different person. I almost didn't recognize him. Is he letting you and Charlie stay in the house?"

"I think he will! Olivia has convinced him to let me stay. He stays by himself a lot, and I leave food for him in the refrigerator. But, I don't think he wants any company right now."

"I am glad you and Charlie are staying here, especially if I get to stay longer. It would be so much fun to have Christmas with you both." Ella Rose and Charlie were rolling a ball back and forth while talking.

"I am not sure Charlie will know what is going on. But, I know she will love the Christmas tree lights and learn how to rip open presents. I enjoyed it also when I was a kid."

"If I am here longer, I could help with the festival also."

"That's a great idea. I will keep an eye out at the church. Would late Saturday morning be okay to watch Charlie? I could put her down for a nap, and you could play with her after she wakes up. I would only be at the church for about three hours."

"I will come over around 11:00 and can stay for as long as you want. "

Emma hugged Ella Rose and said she would see her then. After that, it was time for their afternoon walk, so Emma and Charlie followed Ella Rose outside.

Michael had heard Emma leave when the front door closed. He opened his door and went downstairs. He realized he needed to get cleaned up, but his fatigue was overwhelming. Just going downstairs was a challenge. He opened the refrigerator door and saw a left-over turkey leg. It had always been a favorite of his as a child. As he leaned back against the counter, he chewed around the bone without heating it. It tasted delicious to him, and he washed it down with a big drink of water. He wiped his face with a towel and threw the turkey bone into the trash.

Looking in the mirror yesterday, he had realized how much weight he had lost in the past few weeks. The trip back from Afghanistan through Germany was an uncomfortable ordeal. The transport airplanes were undoubtedly not first class, but they got him home quickly. He hardly remembered the trip but realized he had been in shock until his last days in Germany. Yet, looking around the kitchen, he felt it looked better than it ever had before.

The little housekeeper had been doing a good job, but he would rather be alone. If Emma were not here, his mother would be on his case all the time. That would be worse. He loved his mother, but he didn't want to share anything with anybody right now. He went back upstairs to another rough night of trying to sleep.

CHaPTer SIXTeen

...in which Charlie and Emma bring
Christmas to Michael's home

I t was still almost a month before Christmas, but Emma searched through Michael's house, hoping she would find Christmas decorations. When Charlie fell asleep for her morning nap, Emma decided to go into the attic to look in stored boxes. It was a little dusty, but Michael organized the boxes well. Luckily they were by the gable windows, which provided light to see inside the boxes. She couldn't resist going to the gable window that reminded her of one in her attic. Emma had lovely memories of being a teenager, putting a pillow on the frame, and wondering about her future. She would wish on a first star she saw that something good would happen to her. Emma remembered even praying for a white Christmas one year but couldn't recall if it happened.

Emma noticed that the days between Thanksgiving and Christmas started to fly by with all the holiday preparations. Of course, living in Hill Brook with their long-standing tradition of a Christmas festival made it go even faster. But, it seemed to be fun compared with her childhood memories.

The first box she opened had files and old records. The second container had many photographs. She hated to pry into Michael's life, but she was still curious about it. There were cute pictures of him in his baseball uniform, Halloween costumes, and one of him and another young boy.

Emma wondered who he was. She turned the photo over. But, of course, there were no names. She thought to herself; most people forget to write people's names and the date on photographs. It looked as if the two boys were terrific friends. She would like to talk to Olivia about his childhood. The last album showed photos of an older Michael with a younger African American man. Michael was carrying a backpack, and the younger man had a video camera. Emma wondered where they were and why they were there. The background in the photo looked like a foreign country. She sighed and realized there probably were no Christmas decorations in the attic. Maybe she could check the basement during the next nap that Charlie took.

As Emma climbed down from the attic, she wondered when Charlie would start to outgrow one of her naps. She thought about how her sister would never know about her. She wished her sister could see her grow up. It was not to be

The next day, she spent Charlie's afternoon nap in the basement looking through Michael's boxes. She noticed a closet lined with cedar where he stored clothes. He was one organized person, and Emma wondered if he had done the construction himself. She found several boxes with decorations for a Christmas tree. There seemed to be little else to decorate the house. She thought it would be fun to decorate the front porch with twinkling lights. Emma had seen some light sets for sale at the market. She wondered how hard it would be to hang but thought she could call Joe. He would know the best way to use the lights without damaging Michael's porch. She certainly didn't want to upset him more than he was. Emma called Joe and left a message on his answering machine that she would need help with a holiday project. After Thanksgiving, he had come over the weekend to rake the backyard. Emma hadn't mentioned that Michael was home.

Joe called back later that day, and she told him that she wanted lights for the front porch. He offered to pick them up at the market and come over immediately. But, unfortunately, he had no jobs until Saturday.

A little later that afternoon, Elizabeth stopped by to see how Emma was doing. They sat in the living room, talking when they heard a knock on the door. Elizabeth and Emma both went to the door. Emma was holding Charlie.

"Hi Joe, thanks for doing this for me. You remember Elizabeth Turner?"

Joe answered with a nod and said, "Nice to see you again."

"Same to you. You did a great job on my counter. I might need some more bookshelves soon if you are available."

"I can come by next week and see what you have in mind." Joe said as he turned to Emma and asked if she had a step stool; his ladder wouldn't work. She got one from the closet while he tested the lights. He thought a few small nails would hold the tiny lights. They stood at the front door with Charlie to watch Joe put up the Christmas lights. The noise of the hammer concerned Emma, hoping it wouldn't disturb Michael.

Joe was working quickly, but not necessarily quietly. Then, finally, Michael came down the stairs. "What is going on down here?"

"I am sorry, Michael. Joe is putting up lights on the porch for the holidays. I didn't think you would mind."

"I just couldn't figure out what the noise was." He went out on the porch in his bare feet and said, "Hi Joe. Are you having fun?"

Joe looked down and was surprised to see Michael and said, "Whoa, I didn't know you were back. Emma asked me to put up the lights. I think she likes the holidays."

"No problem. Emma is my housekeeper and has the run of the house. Mom gave her a year contract. Aren't I lucky?" he said while turning to face Emma, who blushed.

"Michael, this is Elizabeth Turner, who owns the bookstore in town," she said as she turned to Elizabeth.

"Are you here to decorate the house?" he asked sarcastically, not recognizing her from high school.

"No, just visiting."

Joe continued hanging the lights while Michael went into the house and back upstairs without talking to Emma.

"That went well!" she said to herself under her breath. She felt that every time Michael talked was encouraging.

When the lights hung, it gave the house a welcoming glow. She carried Charlie and walked out to the sidewalk with Elizabeth to see the effect of the lights. It was amazing what twinkling lights could do for the holidays. She thanked Joe and asked him if he ever helped more people than just Millie and Olivia.

"I do work for both of them, especially Millie with her boarding house. But I do all sorts of work around town."

"That's a good thing. I know the ladies appreciate your work. You know Millie has interesting guests. They all came over for Thanksgiving dinner. We had a great time."

"Did anyone know Michael was coming home?"

"No, everyone was shocked when he came in. I was upstairs with Charlie, and when I came downstairs, he said, "I guess I have to fire you.""

"That's harsh!" Joe said.

"He finally accepted the fact that I have a year contract. He stays by himself most of the time."

"Well, thanks for the extra work. I always like it this time of year."

Emma took money from her wallet to pay him for his time and repay him for the lights.

"Thanks for doing the lights quickly," Emma called as Joe got in his truck and glanced back at Elizabeth.

"That was interesting," Emma said, looking at Elizabeth.

"I don't know what you mean. Joe is just doing a job for me. Nothing more."

"Whatever you say," Emma answered with a chuckle.

CHaPTer seventeen

…in which Ella Rose gets help from an unlikely source

Later that week, Ella Rose came over to Michael's house right on time, and Emma showed her around the house. "Hi Ella Rose. Before I leave, I have an idea of something for your new friends to do before the holidays. My family has always made Gingerbread Houses. I found some kits downtown at Molly's, and I wondered if you might get a few friends to make them. They can bring a bag of candy to share, but I will buy the little kits. They are all ready to be decorated. Would you check with some friends? We could plan an afternoon in December?"

"Sure! I will ask around. How many do you think could come?"

"Well, I think there were at least ten kits at Molly's. Michael's dining room table has enough room for ten."

"It sounds like fun! Are we allowed to eat some of the candy?"

"Sure. That's part of the fun. Let's plan on Thursday, Dec. 20, after school, looking at the calendar. Isn't that the last day of school before the winter break?"

"It is. I will check around. None of my friends are going out of town this year. Thanks, Emma! You are nice to find fun things for the holidays."

"Thanks! Just seeing the whirligigs around town have helped me with my Christmas spirit."

Together, they went up the stairs where Charlie was still sleeping and probably would sleep a little longer. Emma told Ella Rose where Charlie's afternoon snack was and the toys in the living room. Emma showed her where she kept the diapers and wipes.

"A couple of my friends and I took a babysitting course at a Kansas City hospital. Changing diapers was one of the most important lessons. After that, we practiced on dolls, and I bet Charlie will not lay as quietly."

Emma laughed and said, "I just keep a firm hand on her tummy, and she is pretty good."

"Thanks for the good advice. I brought a book. I will sit here in the rocker and read until Charlie wakes up."

"Thanks for doing this. I think Michael is asleep or just in his room. I doubt he will come out while you are here."

"No problem. Have a good time with the sisters. Aren't they a pair? Do you know they used to teach in the same school for years? Grandma told me neither married, but they are the happiest people. I love that they still dress somewhat alike."

"I agree. The sisters are such fun! Maybe they will show me how to make something useful today," Emma said as she left the room.

"Have fun!" Ella Rose sat in the rocking chair by Charlie's crib. She was reading a book she brought but would read Whirligig next, which Emma had recommended. Charlie woke with a smile and seemed to look around for Emma. She puckered up a little before Ella Rose picked her up. Charlie looked toward the bedroom door, probably looking for Emma. Ella Rose wisely distracted her by showing her a little teddy bear that she had brought over as a gift for her charge. She laughed and grabbed it.

Ella Rose decided Charlie needed her diaper changed. She found everything she needed on the little chest Emma used as a changing table. As predicted, Charlie wanted no part of it. She decided it was more fun to spin around, twisting and turning. She laughed at Ella Rose's attempt to hold her down.

"Need some help?" came a deep voice from the doorway.

Both Charlie and Ella Rose were startled and turned their heads to see who was talking.

Charlie turned her head away shyly, but Ella Rose nodded and said, "Yes! Could you hold her down, gently, of course?"

"Sure," he said. Michael came over slowly and gently put his hand on her stomach and started talking to her quietly. "Are you a little trouble-maker, Miss Charlie?" he said as he smiled. "Are you ready? Move fast," he said to Ella Rose.

She wasted no time. She removed the soiled diaper, cleaned Charlie up, and put on a clean diaper. "Thanks," she said as she wiped her hands with the hand sanitizers.

"I think I remember you," Michael said as he looked at Ella Rose. "Aren't you the Dolan's granddaughter?"

"Yes, I am staying with them while my parents are in Europe on a business trip."

"Nice of you to babysit Charlie. Where is Emma?"

"She went to the church to help with the festival preparations."

"Ah, Christmas must be coming," Michael said, shrugging his shoulders. "Are you okay now with her?"

"I think we need a snack. What do you think, Charlie?"

Charlie started bobbing around in Ella Rose's arms. "Well, let's go," Ella Rose said, heading out the door. "Thanks again for your help. I hope we didn't disturb you too much. Emma said that you needed quiet."

"No, I am okay," Michael said, looking out the window of the bedroom. He subconsciously rubbed his shoulder while looking out the window. The pain and the bruise on his stomach still felt sore, but the black and blue marks were fading. The discomfort was mild next to the pain he felt in his heart. Michael turned back to his bedroom with a glance back at Charlie and Ella Rose.

Emma left the house, smiling and thinking this was nice to be away from home for just a while. "I need to relax a little, and it is nice to get away from the house where the feeling is tense," she thought to herself.

She walked quickly to the church and saw a door to the educational wing. She could hear voices coming from the basement. She went down the stairs to smell fresh coffee, and she thought donuts.

"Hi, Emma," called Mary Margaret, sitting behind a sewing machine.

"Hi Mary Margaret, what are you making?"

"I am piecing together quilt squares. We are making a Christmas quilt to raffle off during the festival. This year we are making a pattern called Whirlwind. It reminds us of the whirligigs that John makes. It is nice to keep a tradition going. Would you like to cut out the pieces for us? I have the patterns to use and also very sharp scissors."

"I think I could do that. Maybe someone should show me first how best to do it, and then I could follow."

"Esther Marie, could you show Emma how to cut out pieces for the quilt?"

"Of course, always a teacher!"

Emma had an enjoyable few hours, getting to know more people from Hill Brook and learning how to cut pieces for a quilt. It was essential to cut them carefully so the patterns fit together.

After an hour or so, Esther Marie turned off the sewing machine light and said, "Let's take a break for coffee and maybe a donut."

Emma thought she and her sister seemed to be the team leaders, at least for the quilt raffle. There were six sewing machines in the craft room. The frame for the actual quilting was in a corner. Emma had never seen how to quilt, so the next couple of weeks would be fascinating.

"The donuts come from The Coffee Bean and Chicken Café," Esther Marie said.

"That's the first place I went to when I came to town. I fell in love with the chicken and dumplings."

"That Nelly Blanding is a marvel. She can cook anything. I love that she let her grandchildren name the café. Everybody thinks it is a great name," admitted Esther Marie. Josh's sister, Rebecca, encouraged her children to come up with a clever name."

Emma chuckled and said, "I also love that the hardware store's name uses alliteration."

Mary Margaret came up and added, "Do you know that his full name is Harley Hardman, but everyone told him not to use his full name in the store's name. That would have been a mouthful."

Emma laughed before taking a chocolate-long john donut. She had always had a fondness for the long donut covered with chocolate. "I haven't had a donut in so long, and these look wonderful." After taking a bite, she said, "They are fresh, and the coffee is delicious, but I need to go pretty soon to relieve Ella Rose, who is watching Charlie for me. She is such a nice girl but seemed lonely being alone with her grandparents. I am glad they enrolled her at Truman Middle School as her parents will not return soon."

Esther Marie took a sip of coffee and then said, "I hate to ask, but how is Michael doing? We were so worried after Thanksgiving and his coming home out of the blue. Do you know he was in my sixth-grade class about twenty years ago? Smart as a tack, but a little quiet. He could be a trickster also. We almost didn't recognize him when he came back on Thanksgiving," admitted Esther Marie.

"I think he is getting rest, spending most of his time in his room. He may go out sometimes, but I don't hear him if he does."

Emma stood up and put her cup in the tray marked for used dishes. It looked like the church was trying to be environmentally aware by using china cups. She was glad they were not using Styrofoam. "Thanks to both of you for letting me join the plans for the festival."

She headed back to Michael's house, feeling very productive about having helped with the quilt raffle. She took the shortest way back to

Michael's. As she turned the corner, a black sedan drove by very slowly. The front side windows were tinted so that Emma couldn't see inside, but she felt chills down her spine. Instinctively, she looked down and turned slightly away from the car. She thought that it was odd that the car was going slowly.

Emma finally looked up to see the car turn onto the next street. It did not drive by again. She was grateful that she could go through the front door with no one on the road. Emma was pleased to see Ella Rose and Charlie playing on the floor as she closed the door. Because Ella Rose remembered that little children love repetitive games, they were playing Peek a Boo repeatedly.

Charlie looked up and saw Emma put out her arms to her. She bounced up and down. "Hi, Peanut! Are you having fun with Ella Rose?" It looked as if they were having a great time. "Thank you so much, Ella Rose."

"Did you have a good time, Ms. Morrison?"

"Oh, please call me, Emma," she said, smiling. "I had a great time, and I am learning how to make a quilt. I am so glad I will be here for the holidays."

"My dad just called my grandmother and said they definitely wouldn't be back until after the New Year. I am excited that the school in Hill Brook let me enroll so I don't lose time in eighth grade. I would love to be involved with the Christmas Eve pageant at the church."

"I know everyone will love you," Emma said as she reached for her wallet to give Ella Rose payment for her babysitting. "Thanks again for your time."

"Michael helped me change Charlie's diaper. You were right. She loves to twist and turn. He helped by holding her tummy. He seemed sadder than tired, though. He remembered me from other times I visited my grandparents. I loved every minute of being with Charlie. Thank you for the money. I would love to have some cash to buy my grandparents something for Christmas."

"That's very thoughtful," Emma said as she picked Charlie up and walked Ella Rose to the front door. Emma watched as she ran next door. She couldn't help but look up and down the street to see if the same car came back around. It was unnerving to think a detective had found her. She thought she would have to be careful and watch for herself, especially when she went anywhere in town.

CHAPTER EIGHTEEN

...in which Emma visits a fairyland of whirligigs

During the first week of December, Emma remained respectful of the house's silence but wished she could play Christmas music. She loved all the Johnny Mathis' Christmas albums and knew there were lots of CDs in Michael's bookcase. He had quite a collection of all types of CDs. Maybe if he went out for a walk or something, she could play songs for Charlie's second Christmas. She was determined to have an enjoyable holiday for Charlie.

One morning, Emma decided to bake Christmas cookies for tradition's sake and lure Michael out of his room. She loved to make the shortbread pecan cookies her grandmother used to make. The butter in them made them taste creamy. She always got to roll them in powdered sugar when she was a child and got it all over her clothes. She chuckled at the good memories.

They were in the kitchen; Charlie was watching her mother rolling the cookies in her highchair. Emma gave her plain sugar cookies, but the pecan cookies would be great to give to Olivia, Millie, and neighbors for gifts. Just then, someone knocked on the back door.

"Hi, John, welcome. I just made some Christmas cookies. Would you like some? I can always make more."

"I would enjoy it," he said, pulling out a chair and tweaking Charlie's nose, who giggled. "This room smells great. My wife used to make cookies every Christmas. I gained five pounds every year and tried to take them off in January," he said as he patted his stomach.

"I even have some real cocoa to go with the cookies," Emma said, stirring cocoa into some warm milk.

"You are going to spoil us with all these treats," he teased. "They are delicious," he said with powdered sugar all over his chin.

Charlie was laughing at them both.

"I have been worried about Michael since Thanksgiving. I haven't seen him outside for days. Has he gone anywhere?"

"He came down the afternoon when Joe installed the lights on the porch but didn't say much. I haven't seen him leave. Charlie and I have taken walks in the mornings and afternoons to give him some space. He might be going out then. Although I know Michael eats the food, I leave him in the refrigerator. I wish I knew how to help him. Something severe must have happened where he was assigned. He might have Post Traumatic Stress Disorder, even though he was not a soldier."

"He was mostly a serious kid, but sometimes he showed a great sense of humor. He had quite a few friends and was very athletic."

Changing the subject, John said, "I invited Walter and Monroe over to work on some whirligigs later this week and wondered if you and Charlie would like to come over right now and see my workshop. Unfortunately, there would be too much sawdust for Charlie to come later when the others work on them. I am going to Kansas City to pick up some supplies I use in making the whirligigs, but I will be back later in the day."

"We would enjoy seeing your workshop, John." She paused a moment before she said, "I have a favor to ask you. I can't explain it, but I wondered if you would call a number for me from Kansas City and let it ring four times. It is important. If you could find a public telephone somewhere, that would be perfect."

"I had a notion you might be having some issues, but there is something about you that I trust. I will be glad to do that. I think there is an old phone booth near my supplier. Do you have the number?"

She handed him a small piece of neatly folded paper. "I appreciate it. If you could keep it to yourself, I would be grateful."

Now it was her turn to change the subject. "We would love to see your workshop. So let me change Charlie, and we will be right over."

Emma walked over to John's house with Charlie on her hip and knocked on his basement door.

"The door is open!"

Emma felt like she was in fairyland with all kinds of whirligigs hanging everywhere in all phases of being finished. Cutouts in pieces ready to be painted lay on the counter, and others were ready to be sanded. John told her many Whirligigs were not put on poles yet but would be before they sold.

"I just finished one with a Christmas tree. A little boy and girl decorate it when the propellers turn. My favorites are the ones that have parts that move when the propellers rotate with the wind."

Charlie turned a whirligig propeller that looked like a mermaid moving up and down in the waves. Emma laughed and thought the construction of the whirligigs was terrific. "You are quite an artist, John! These are beautiful."

"I have always loved making things. But, since Helen died, I have found making these has given me a real purpose."

"You know, John, I remembered that when I was in eighth grade, my English teacher had Writers' Workshops. I found I enjoyed thinking of stories to write and share. Ella Rose and her new friends have joined together for a writing club. I wondered if you would talk about how you got involved with making whirligigs and what it has done for you. Even the teens in Hill Brook know the town has become famous for the whirligigs you make. Writing memories help us to realize truths in our lives."

"Let's see how well the preparations for the festival go. I am sure I can squeeze in an hour or two. But, first, I would like to hear what the teens are writing about now. Life for teenagers has to be different than when I was in school," John said as he walked with Emma and Charlie to the door.

"Thanks for inviting Morris and Walter over this week. I hope they enjoy your company and the chance to do something fun."

"Thanks for the suggestion. I will let you know how it goes this week."

"Bye, John," Emma said while Charlie waved at him as they left.

chapter nineteen

...in which Michael teases Emma about
being the town matchmaker

The days blurred into another while Emma tried to be quiet for Michael and yet let Charlie be an active little child. Emma felt she owed her time to be herself. Charlie was not aware of what she had lost. Who said life was fair? Things don't always go the way we want them to, but we need to adjust and move on. Easy to say, hard to do, she thought.

All the church ladies, including Mary Margaret and Esther Marie, welcomed Charlie to the church basement. They found a little portable crib and gave her toys from the church nursery to keep her occupied. Emma was becoming very good at cutting out the pieces of the whirlwind pattern. The ladies showed her how to piece them together, so Esther Marie and Mary Margaret could sew them. Many in the group were good with a needle. Emma's mother had taught her and her sister how to sew some basic projects, but they had never done any quilting.

Everyone was friendly and always asked about Michael, although Emma had very little to say. She worried that he wouldn't get over whatever was bothering him from his time in the Middle East. Olivia called him often. Although he would answer the phone, he only said okay.

Emma had heard him leave the house several times after she went to bed but didn't know when he came home. She hoped he didn't sit at a bar and drink.

"Oh, I forgot to tell you. Ella Rose will stay in Hill Brook for the rest of the semester. Pat told me that her parents are having trouble getting a license for their export business and are staying in Europe a little longer. They won't come home before the first of the year."

"How is she doing with the news?" Mary Margaret asked Emma.

"Well, she is excited about being back in school, even a new school. I think she is a good student and loves to read and learn."

"I think the kids at Truman Middle School are friendly, but that age can have cliques. However, I have met some of them at the writing club, and they seem to care about each other."

"Hi Emma," said a woman Emma had not yet met. "My name is Mildred Hoxie. I have a granddaughter at that school in the eighth grade. I wonder if they have met. What is her name again?"

"Ella Rose," answered Emma. "She would be thrilled to meet another student at the school."

"I think my granddaughter, Margaret, who we call Maggie, and her friends are very nice and will include her in their activities."

"I met her at the café. Is she working there part-time?"

"She just works the late afternoon shift, already thinking about college and saving money."

"I am happy you think she will welcome Ella Rose. It is hard to be the new kid in school. Well, Charlie and I better hit the road. I might be able to get her to take an afternoon nap." She touched the top of the quilt pieces gently. "I love the way the quilt is taking shape."

"We will start quilting tomorrow. Esther Marie and I will set it up on the frame tonight, and the quilters will come for the next week to finish up. I am sure they would be happy to teach you how to quilt."

"I would enjoy that. Learning new things is fun." Emma said as she and Charlie got their coats on and left the church basement.

Walking home, Emma felt a little tense. She kept talking to Charlie about what they were passing. She had developed a habit of looking around suspiciously, although she had not seen another slowly moving black car. Then, finally, Emma turned and noticed Amy running toward her.

"Hi Emma," said Amy as she hurried to catch up with her. "Are you headed home? What did you think of the book, Whirligig?"

"So good to see you, Amy! I loved it! Although it was sad, it is encouraging to see that the boy recovered from a traumatic experience."

"The library only has one copy, so I thought I might get it back from you. Do you mind? I would like to read it myself."

"Sure, we are headed back to Michael's house right now."

"Hi Charlie," Amy said, leaning down and patting her head. "She is so cute."

They walked down the main street quietly, but Emma turned to ask, "How are you settling in Hill Brook? Are you looking for an apartment?"

"Yes, I love staying at mom's but would like to find a place of my own. I've just been so busy organizing the library. I found out it is woefully behind the times. They have very few computers, and Wi-Fi access is poor. I talked to the library board soon to encourage more funds. Technology is developing so fast, and I love what it can do."

"I agree. Good Luck with that."

They both spotted the police car outside Michael's home as they turned the corner. Emma was nervous but thought Amy would love to run into Josh and Michael. On the other hand, Emma dreaded running into the police officers after Harrison tried to ask her more questions than she wanted to answer. Could they be inside talking to Michael? The older police officer had told her that he and Michael had gone to school together. Wasn't his name Blanding? She tried to remember.

As she opened the unlocked front door, the three men were standing in the living room just talking. Michael had made no effort to have them sit down.

"Hello, Ms. Morrison, how are you?" Chief Blanding asked.

"I am fine," she answered. "But, please call me Emma."

Charlie turned her face into Emma's shoulder, with the three prominent men standing right in front of her.

Amy turned to Josh and said with a twinkle in her eye, "Good to see you, Chief Blanding! It's been a while since I have seen you. Congratulations on your promotion. And hi Michael, so glad you are back in town." She turned to the other officer and said, "I don't believe we have met; I am Amy Perkins. I just became the new town librarian."

"Good to meet you," said the younger officer, blushing. "I am Harrison."

Josh leaned over and hugged her. "Glad you are back, Amy."

Michael said, "Hi Amy," but didn't offer a hug.

Josh looked at Emma and said, "We remember many things from our high school days, I think!"

"We just met walking, and I am returning a book to Amy. Would you hold Charlie while I find the book?" Emma asked Amy.

"Of course."

Josh said, "What book are you both reading?"

"Emma remembered a book titled, Whirligig when she was in school. Since Hill Brook is swimming in whirligigs, she thought it a good idea to reread it."

"Sounds interesting!" Josh added.

Emma returned with the book and took Charlie back in her arms. "Well, this little lady is headed for a nap. It is good to see you again, Amy. Maybe we can meet sometime and discuss the book? " Suddenly, Emma thought of the conversation she had with her at the library the first day they met. "Did you guys know that Hill Brook Library is technologically outdated?"

"No, I haven't been there recently," answered Josh. "What do you have in mind?"

"I'm not sure. Maybe Amy has thought about it. Do you have any ideas, Amy?"

Amy shook her head and said, "I went to the Library board first, and they said there was no money in the current budget but could do something in a couple of years. Regrettably, I can't tell you how old the computers are now. I have tried for some grants but haven't heard back."

"Sounds like a good start, but there might be grants just for technology," offered Harrison.

"Good to know," Amy answered.

"Maybe we could sponsor some fundraiser. For example, there is a new winery just outside town. Maybe they would sponsor something to let the town know about their business," suggested Josh.

"That sounds like fun," added Emma. "What do you think, Amy?"

"I like that," she answered.

"Maybe, Amy, we could get together for coffee and talk about it," Josh suggested.

"That would be great! Come by the library tomorrow around 10:30 am. I have a new coffee pot, and we can brainstorm then," Amy said, smiling at Josh.

Michael said nothing during this conversation, but he looked over at Emma, curious at the exchange.

"Bye, gentlemen," Amy said as Emma walked her new friend to the door. Amy turned and winked at Emma.

Charlie was still acting shy with the three tall men and tucked her head into Emma's shoulder.

"And how is your little one?" Josh asked in a friendly manner.

"She is fine, but now it's time for her nap," Emma said, heading for the stairs.

Harrison said nothing, but she felt his eyes watching her as she went upstairs. She could hear them murmuring. Then she heard the front door close and looked out the window in her room and saw them pull away.

Emma removed Charlie's coat and settled her into the crib. She had had a busy afternoon with all the ladies fussing over her at the church.

While Charlie was on her back, she hugged her favorite stuffed toy John had given her on Thanksgiving. Then, finally, she seemed to sleep better, cuddled up with it. Emma sat in the rocking chair, watching as Charlie fell asleep. She saw her eyes closing and rocked her slightly. The light outside was fading because clouds had been developing all day. Emma didn't think it was cold enough for snow today, but maybe for Christmas this year. It was always special when it snowed on Christmas as a little girl. The holidays were pleasant, but the snow made it even better.

Emma's eyes opened to see that Charlie was asleep, but she was startled to see Michael standing in the doorway leaning on the doorframe. He was staring at Charlie in her crib.

"Why were the police officers here today?" she asked, dreading the answer. She hoped they were not looking into her past.

"Josh had heard I was back and wondered how I was doing."

"Did you tell them you hardly ever come out of your room?"

"It isn't any of their business what I do," he responded sharply.

"I'm sorry. I shouldn't have said that. Your friends came by right before Thanksgiving, wondering what I was doing in your house. I liked Chief Blanding and had met Harrison at the market."

"I don't know him, but Josh and I have known each other since high school."

Emma wasn't about to share why she was concerned about the officers' interest in her background. She needed to keep it a secret for a little longer. She hoped she could check in with her parents soon.

"Are you okay?" Michael asked as he noticed her faraway look.

"Sure!" she said, looking back at him. Not much she could share with anyone about her situation. It was a leap of faith that she had asked John to call her parents' phone number without any explanation.

"Listen," Michael said, looking at the ground. "I am sorry how I acted on Thanksgiving. I was just startled to see so many people in the house when I expected it to be dark."

"It's okay. I was just as surprised to see you." She didn't want him to know that she was worried about losing a place to live and a job.

"I need to see my doctor sometime in a day or two. I haven't seen a doctor since I returned and need to be sure I didn't pick up anything from overseas." He wasn't about to mention his bruises. "I had all the shots I needed before I left, but you never know. By the way, my car is in the garage. You can use it whenever you want."

"Thank you," Emma said, staring at his back as he turned to his room. "As long as the weather is good, we like our walks, but I will keep it in mind."

"So, did you arrange that visit today for Amy to meet Josh again after all these years?" Michael asked.

"Not really. It was just good fortune that I met Amy going home from shopping. She wanted to get the book back, but maybe she wanted to see you."

"We knew each other in high school but lost touch when she went to college and got a job at a community college library. My mom let me know where everyone was from our class. You might become the Hill Brook matchmaker, Emma," he said, which sounded like teasing.

"Well, I know what it is like to be lonely, and if two people find each other, so all the better."

"Well, have a good night," he said, turning around.

She was surprised he had spoken to her so easily. Maybe he was doing better than everyone thought.

CHAPTer TWenTY

...in which Emma changes her opinion of a man

E mma decided she and Charlie would walk downtown to buy Christmas gifts the next day. She appreciated getting paid to take care of a beautiful house. The owner wasn't such an ogre and had seemed rather lovely last night. She hoped the doctor could help him, even if he weren't ready to get help.

She decided to stop by Millie's house, hoping to run into Walter and Monroe to see if they were looking forward to working with John. She didn't think she would tell Millie and Olivia about Michael seeing the doctor. She thought he might have malaria or something, but that's a disease from jungle areas. Of course, it might be something else, but he didn't want her mother to worry.

"Hi, Millie," Emma said, walking into her kitchen.

"Hello, girls. I just baked Olivia's favorite recipe, Almond Cranberry Coffee Cake, a recipe from my pastor. It is fairly easy, and the aroma when cooking is wonderful."

Emma stepped into the kitchen and smiled. "That is a great smell. But, then again, I adore almond in anything."

Millie got quiet after cutting squares for each of them and making tea. She gave Charlie a little sugar cookie. "Emma, a man stopped by the house yesterday and asked if a young woman with a baby had stayed at my B and B recently."

Emma felt her face grow hot, and she put down her cup. "What did he look like?" she asked.

"He was at least fifty, rather shabby, and hadn't shaved in a while."

"What did you tell him? "

"Well, I believe the people who stay here deserve my discretion. I told him I never share the names of my guests. A hotel would not either. So I didn't invite him inside and closed the door in his face."

This conversation unnerved Emma, but she tried not to show it. "I appreciate the way you handled it. I am sorry I cannot share what is going on in my life yet. I need to figure it out myself."

"Both Olivia and I decided we would give you time to do just that. We didn't plan on Michael returning early. I am glad he is going to the doctor. I guess Olivia knows. I think she calls him every day but tries not to interfere with what he needs to do for himself."

Emma was able to take a few bites of the coffee cake and asked Millie if she would copy the recipe for her. Reluctantly, she didn't share that her mother would have loved to have it.

They left Millie's. Emma looked up and down the street for a black car out of caution. Maybe that man had been looking around all the roads. Why would he have known where to look? She had been careful not to use a traceable phone. The phone call to her parents hadn't gone through because she hung up after four rings.

They headed to Harley's Hill Brook Hardware Store to look at the finished whirligigs that John had made. Maybe one of them would work as a gift to Olivia. Perhaps she could design one and have John make it just for her. Emma smiled to herself, thinking that would be a special gift.

Charlie enjoyed sitting in her stroller, waving to people on the sidewalks. Most of them stopped to pat her on the head. The friendliness would never happen in her town back east. The cheerful bell over the hardware store's front door rang as they walked inside. The Christmas decorations were attractive, just like the rest of the store. There were rows and rows of actual hardware items, but the store also stocked lots of gift items.

"Hello, may I help you find something?" asked the man behind the counter.

"Hi, I am Emma, and this is Charlie. We are friends of Olivia Williams and John Evans. I am housesitting at her son's house." She didn't share that he was back because she wasn't sure he wanted everyone to know.

"I heard Mike had come back early. Josh Blanding came in a little bit ago and told me he had spoken to him. I hope everything is okay. He does these crazy assignments all over the world and writes about them. I envy his adventurous nature, but I am happy here. By the way, I am Harley Hardeman. Glad to meet you."

"I like that you sell hardware and gifts, especially the whirligigs. Each one of them is unique."

"John can't keep up with the demand."

"I think Walter and Monroe from the B and B will help him during the holidays."

"That's great! Let me know if I can find anything for you two."

"Thanks, Mr. Hardeman!"

"Please, call me Harley; everyone does."

"I'll do that, Harley," she said as they moved down the first aisle.

The store stocked many products for bird watchers. There were tall barrels of different kinds of bird seeds. Emma thought that might be an excellent gift for the sisters. The next aisle had small bird feeders made like houses. They were adorable. Emma picked up one to see the price.

"Are you a bird watcher, Ms. Morrison?" asked a voice behind her.

Emma turned and saw Josh Blanding with a plunger in his hand.

"Problem at the police station?" she asked with a smile.

"Oh, no, my mother owns and manages the café. So she asked me to pick it up. But, unfortunately, the restaurant is always having drain problems."

"Good to know that she has you to help her."

"Hi Charlie, how are you?" he asked, bending down, knowing she couldn't reply.

However, she smiled at him and babbled a few syllables, almost sounding like 'bye, bye.'

"Well, I best be on my way, or my mother will be calling me. You take care."

"You, too, Josh!"

As Josh was about to leave, an older man came up behind Emma. "Hi, Josh, what's up? Got plumbing troubles?" he said.

"Harry, no, just the café. Mom is always having issues with drainage. She is going to have to get a plumber to help her," Josh laughed, waving the plunger.

Harry turned to face Emma and had a puzzled look on his face. "Do I know you?" he said, scratching his forehead.

"Hello, Harry. We met the first day I came to Hill Brook. I remember you recommended The Coffee Bean and Chicken Café. Charlie and I loved it. We are staying in Hill Brook as a housekeeper for Michael Williams' home." She didn't mention that he returned so quickly.

"Glad you stayed in our quaint little town. It is friendly but also has lots of things to do, especially at Christmas time."

"I am already busy with the quilt project at the church. So I learned how to quilt and manage a thimble at the same time."

Harry turned to Josh and said, "I am going the way of the café and would be glad to drop the plunger off for you, Josh."

Josh handed him the tool and said, "I appreciate that! I need to check in with the station."

When Harry left, Josh turned to Emma and said, "I think he is sweet on my mom. They've both been lonely since their spouses died a couple of years ago." He winked and walked quickly toward the door.

Emma thought that it was sweet of Josh to feel that way about his mother, but it was odd that Josh didn't ask about Michael. He stopped by just the other day. They might be talking on the phone sometimes.

She decided to purchase two bird feeder-like houses, which were too cute to pass up. Next, Emma went past another display of Santa carvings, each one more adorable than the next.

She immediately remembered their fireplace mantel at home, where her mother put her enormous collection of Santa figures. She started the group when many of her students gave her unusual Santa ornaments as Christmas presents. After that, everyone gave her different kinds. She had farmers, chefs, and even a mooning Santa if you turned him around. Of course, Emma and Susie were always doing that when guests came to the house. Everyone would laugh. She wanted to purchase a carved Santa figure; she only bought the birdhouses.

She headed back to Michael's house with a careful eye on the streets. She thought that living life like this could not go on forever. But, first, she would have to figure a way out of the fix she was in with Charlie.

CHapTer TwenTY-one

...in which a king breaks the ice and a
snowstorm change everything

E arly the following evening, Emma was in the kitchen after taking
Charlie on their usual afternoon walk and putting her down for a late
nap. Suddenly, she heard a noise from the living room. She peeked in
through the butler's pantry. Emma saw Michael sitting in a corner chair
reading the paper. She hadn't noticed him when she had come in through
the front hall.

He looked up when she said, "I didn't see you in here."

"I found the morning paper and thought I should catch up,"
he responded.

"I hope you have been able to rest. Charlie and I have been trying to
be quiet. We have been taking walks in the mornings and the afternoons."

"You don't have to be quiet. I know there is a lot to do as a housekeeper. I have been eating the food you leave for me." He folded the newspaper and looked out the front window. "Maybe I could eat at a reasonable
time rather than the middle of the night," he said.

Emma thought he looked pale and drawn. There were dark circles
under his eyes. None of that interfered with his handsomeness. Emma
hadn't originally thought of him that way. She was too afraid the night he
returned that he would fire her.

"Of course. I have leftover turkey from Thanksgiving in a casserole in the freezer but could get it ready to go in the oven. I hope that will be okay."

"Sure. I am used to meals on the run, so that will be good."

Emma looked at the knife in her hand and said, "I am making a salad."

She immediately thought she was making small talk, so Emma quickly turned and went back into the kitchen, rolling her eyes. Why am I so tongue-tied? As she finished the salad, she could hear Charlie start making noises. So she headed upstairs.

"Hello, Charlie, ready for dinner? Let's get you cleaned up and head downstairs. We are eating with Michael, although I am unsure what I should call him. It would seem even more awkward to call him Mr. Williams. We might be close in age, but I live in his home. Yikes, why I am explaining this to you. Let's head down after changing you to a clean outfit."

After getting Charlie into the highchair, she put out the warm rolls, the salad, and the Turkey a la King that smelled just like her mother's dish from years. Then, finally, she called into the living room, "What would you like to drink, Michael?"

"Water is fine!" he answered, putting down the newspaper and walking to the kitchen. He stopped for a minute and leaned against the doorframe. It was a rather homey feeling. His kitchen had never looked better. The cabinets glowed, and the counters were shiny and clean. Something smelled very good. He was hungry for the first time in a long time.

Charlie looked up at Michael standing in the doorway, then away as she crammed a cracker into her mouth. He decided not to say anything as the little girl looked shy. Instead, he sat down as quietly as he could.

Emma put the hot casserole on the table along with the rolls. She felt better about being in Michael's home under strange circumstances. It was nice to be able to feed him well with his food. Michael took a big forkful of the casserole and a warm roll. "This is good," he said after tasting it but not looking up.

"I am glad," Emma said, feeling grateful for this second chance. Although she was hungry, she felt funny eating in front of this stranger. They ate quietly, and Charlie kept looking back and forth between the two quiet adults as the shy toddler picked up pieces of food to put into her mouth. She also experimented with her little spoon by picking peas in the sauce. Charlie would try to put them on the spoon, then put them in her mouth. Emma couldn't help but smile and giggle a little as she watched her. Michael glanced up. Emma thought she saw a slight smile, but it was fleeting.

When they finished, she started cleaning off the table, and Michael startled her when he spoke, "So, what is your story?"

She turned and leaned back against the sink and said, "I don't have much of a story!"

"There has to be a story."

Emma thought to herself, I guess he wonders about many things that seem unusual since he is a writer. She looked over at Charlie, who had dozed off in her highchair. "I have coffee made if you wouldn't mind waiting while I put her to bed."

"I can wait… I have all the time in the world," Michael said, confusing Emma.

Picking up the toddler, Emma headed for the stairs, wondering what *his* story might be.

Almost half an hour later, Emma returned after getting Charlie ready for bed and waiting for her to drift off to sleep.

"There is pie leftover from the holiday in the freezer. Would you like a slice since you missed having some on Thanksgiving?" she asked, walking into the kitchen. Michael had cleared off the table and started pouring coffee for both of them. She thought that this would seem like a normal situation if it weren't a little unusual.

"Sure," he said, "I would like a piece! Normally Thanksgiving is my favorite holiday of the year, just not this year."

"You are in luck. I froze the rest of the pecan pie," she said, cutting into the pie which Emma had defrosted earlier. She took slices for herself and Michael. She hadn't had dessert the night of Michael's abrupt arrival.

"So, what's your story, Michael? I know you have been in town for a while. I am almost positive I saw you at the café when Charlie and I arrived. Why didn't you come home then? Your mother hadn't heard from you and wasn't even sure where you were."

"I would rather not talk about it," he answered.

"Oh, but you think I want to talk about my life? That seems like a double standard to me. I am sorry I missed Thanksgiving. This pie is good!"

"Pat Dolan made the pies. You have wonderful neighbors, and I already think the world of your mom and Millie. Everyone has been kind. I even made the turkey with the help of your cookbook and advice from the butcher. There is enough turkey in the freezer for sandwiches for weeks. You have a great pantry, and the freezer is still full. Odd, you left it well-stocked when you left." She blushed, thinking she was blathering to keep up the conversation.

"Well, I left rather quickly and wasn't sure how long I would be gone. I am sorry Mom felt overwhelmed by taking care of my house. I wasn't thinking straight when I left. By the way, I know you didn't have a contract for the housekeeper job. I saw John's computer skills all over that "contract" Mom showed me the morning after Thanksgiving."

Emma tried not to give anything away by her facial expression, but she grinned, looking down at her pie.

"Someone must have copied your signature. Mom, Millie, and John really must like you to have you stick around. I thought since it was so close to Christmas, I couldn't kick you out," Michael added. Emma didn't respond. There wasn't anything to say. He got up to pour a little more coffee for both of them and then sat back down. He got up again after glancing out the window, "Oh, the snow is coming down. I don't think they predicted a snowstorm. It is early in the season for this much."

Emma joined him at the window and was shocked to see five inches of snow on the ground and heavy snow continuing. "I guess I should have caught the evening news for the latest prediction." She hadn't realized how close she was standing to him until she looked up into his eyes. She caught her breath and didn't notice how tall and strong he was. But there were still black circles under his tired eyes.

Quickly turning around, she lost her balance. Michael instinctively grabbed her shoulders to help her get her steadiness. Both were a little embarrassed by their closeness, and they immediately stepped back. Michael felt strange touching her. When he let go abruptly, he felt awkward; the fragrance in her hair, like lemons, stayed with him.

Emma cleared the table. Michael said he would shovel the sidewalk before too much more fell that night. "I will probably run over to Mom's house and check on her," he said as he put on his cowboy hat and heavy coat. "You might want to look around for candles just in case we lose power. I put in a battery-operated generator, but it takes a bit to get going. I will be back in about an hour. Millie might need some help also."

As he left the house with the shovel, he was glad that he still had the bandages on his chest. His pain level was much less than it had been while he was recovering in Germany. However, he had to talk to the officers about not contacting his mother after the accident. Michael was not ready to share anything about what had happened in Afghanistan. He caught his breath as he went outside, the snow and ice hitting his face. During his time in the Middle East, it had been hot and humid, so this was a significant change.

The night was so quiet he was afraid that his disturbing thoughts would overtake him again. Nightmares had haunted his nights since the incident, and his eyes showed fatigue. He needed to see his regular doctor, which the doctors in Germany had recommended. Maybe he would call in the next few days. But, instead, he realized he was procrastinating. With the snowflakes flying in his face, he continued to walk through the snowdrifts.

The snow was piling up quickly. He decided to head over to his mother's first. Then, he would come back to do his sidewalk.

When Michael left, Emma closed the back door behind him. She thought he might be quiet and sad, but he was thoughtful, especially about his mother. After he left, Emma went upstairs to see if Charlie was still covered. The upstairs was warm enough, and she left the night-light glowing when she pulled the door nearly shut. She turned on the kitchen radio while cleaning up the dinner dishes and putting leftovers in the refrigerator.

The snow kept falling for the next hour. Finally, when Emma started worrying about Michael being outside, the back door came open. He came through with his coat and hat covered with a coating of snow. "Whew! I haven't seen the snow coming down that fast in a long time. We could be in for a blizzard." He stomped his boots, trying to get off most of the caked-on snow and ice. He pulled them off and then tugged at his socks, which seemed wet also. His nose and cheeks were red. "I should have taken a face stocking. I used to have some in the closet. The temperature has dropped like a rock."

"I made a fire in the fireplace in case we lost power," Emma said as she handed Michael a towel to dry his hair.

"That's good! I wonder if there is any whiskey in the cabinet. I can't remember if I had any when I left last September," he said as he walked through the pantry to check. "Here is some. That will warm me up. Want a little?"

"No, thank you. I stayed inside and felt fine. Come sit by the fire and warm up even more."

Emma sat down on one of the chairs by the side of the fireplace. Michael sat opposite her, close to the fire as he could. Emma could see him shivering and asked, "Could I get you a clean pair of socks while you warm up?"

"That would be good because my feet are still wet and cold."

Emma headed upstairs and found a pair in his chest of drawers. Looking around, she thought she might want to tackle his room and tidy it up. She wondered if his being in the Middle East had thinned his blood. Was that more than just an old wives' tale? She wasn't about to ask him. He seemed okay, but she kept thinking that something must have happened on his assignment to bring him back to the states earlier than he had planned. Also, he acted angry at the people dining on Thanksgiving, and one of the guests was his mother. He was a mystery, no doubt, but she had her secrets preying on her again.

"Here are the warmest socks I could find. Are you warming up?" Emma asked to say something to break the silence, although the silence wasn't so bad.

"My toes are tingling, so the feeling is coming back. If I had frostbite, it would hurt more."

Going against her first thought not to intrude on him, Emma asked, "Could I ask you where you were on assignment recently?"

"I'd rather not talk about it," he said, looking into his drink.

"Of course, I understand."

"Why don't you tell me a little something about yourself," he said. She smiled and replied, "I'd rather not talk about it!"

"Touché!" he responded as his mouth turned up slightly, not exactly in a smile.

It became tranquil again as they both stared into the fire, although Emma rose to put more wood on the fire. "I forgot how comforting a fire could be," she admitted.

Michael didn't say anything. He took another sip, finishing his drink. He got up and went over to look out the front window. "It is still coming down heavily, and I suspect it will continue overnight."

"Will your mom and Millie be okay alone?"

"They are fine. Millie likes to stay close to her residents."

"Well, guess I will go upstairs to bed. Are you going to stay up a little while?" Emma asked as she stood.

"I can wait until the fire dies down a little and close the fireplace glass. Glad the furnace is going strong."

"Well, good night then."

Chapter Twenty-Two

...in which Michael plays nurse and babysitter

Emma didn't fall asleep quickly because she was very curious about Michael's situation. Questions kept intruding on her mind. Why had he returned early? Where had he been assigned? Had he encountered violence? She finally drifted off but was awakened by a shout from somewhere upstairs. At first, she thought it might be Charlie, but it came from down the hallway. She peeked out her bedroom door because the sound seemed to be coming from Michael's room.

"Watch out!"Michael shouted.

Although she was concerned, Emma didn't want to intrude on him during the night. His door was slightly ajar, so she pushed it open and saw Michael tangled up in his blankets. He was sitting up with a wild look in his eyes. It appeared that a nightmare had awakened him. She stood still for a bit, knowing that the streetlights were silhouetting her shape in the doorway.

"Are you okay?" she asked quietly, not sure he was awake.

His head was in his hands, and he rubbed his face and pushed his hair out of his eyes, "Sorry if I woke you."

"No problem. I was worried about you," Emma said.

For a long time, Michael stared at her before saying, "I must have had a nightmare." He didn't add anything more.

"Could I get you a glass of water?"

"No, I am fine now. Go back to bed."

She pulled the door to where it had been when she got there.

"Go ahead and pull it shut."

Doing that, she quietly went back to her room but checked on Charlie before she closed her door.

Emma lay in bed for a while, thinking about Michael and his nightmare. She wished she knew what was bothering him. It must be something that happened on his assignment and why he came home early. It was his story to tell in his time so she wouldn't press him.

The following day Emma peeked in on Charlie, who was still asleep. The snow was falling again, and it was a beautiful sight. When she went downstairs to make coffee, she drank a big glass of water then realized she had a bit of a sore throat. Emma thought she had seen some aspirin in the cabinet. After she found the bottle, she took two. It was not easy to be sick with a young child.

After the coffee perked, she went back upstairs to see if Charlie was awake. She was standing in her crib, looking out the window. It was the first snow she remembered seeing. "Let's get you dressed, Peanut, and maybe we can play in the snow for a bit." She was feeling better after taking the aspirin.

Going downstairs, Emma felt like making waffles. She still remembered the joy of getting an unexpected snow day in school. It changed the rhythm of an ordinary day. Charlie was munching on some Cheerios while the waffles were steaming, and Michael walked in dressed, with his hair combed.

"I haven't seen this much snowfall this early in so long!" Michael said as he looked at Charlie, cramming cereal into her mouth. He didn't say anything, but he did touch her head as he passed to get some coffee.

Emma saw the gesture and thought that Michael wasn't as angry as he seemed before.

That afternoon, Michael went to his mom's house to see how she was doing. He would also check on Millie and her boarders. Unluckily, the snow was still falling. Forecasters said that roads would not melt for a while even though the end was in sight. Emma decided to lie down while Charlie took her nap because her sore throat had not improved. She didn't want to say anything to Michael. She felt like she was a burden as it was.

It was dark when she woke up. She thought she was still dreaming. She felt hot and sick to her stomach. She laid there for a bit and then tried to get up. Charlie still must be sleeping, as Emma heard no noise. She closed her eyes, thinking she would be better in a bit. She drifted off and finally awoke to hear Charlie crying. Then the crying stopped. Emma got up, feeling somewhat shaky, and made her way to the door to Charlie's bedroom. She leaned against the doorjamb and saw Michael murmuring to Charlie. He glanced over his shoulder and could tell that she was not feeling well.

"Whoa, you look a little shaky. Are you okay?" Michael asked as he picked up Charlie, who immediately put her arms out to go to Emma.

"I think I have the flu or something," she replied, still holding onto the doorframe.

Charlie started crying. Michael turned and headed to the hall closet. "I think I have some aspirin up here that isn't out of date. Let me see what we have. You go lay back down."

Emma did as he said and started having chills. What a terrible time to get sick, she thought.

Michael brought the aspirin and a small glass of water to her bedroom, holding onto Charlie like a football. She had stopped crying and laughed at the position as she was looking at the floor.

"Look, Charlie and I can go play downstairs while you rest. I might even be able to give her a snack. I can call the doctor if you aren't better in a bit."

"Sorry to be a bother! I usually never get sick," she said, closing her eyes. She almost laughed when she saw him carrying Charlie that way. It certainly was distracting her and keeping her from crying. It wouldn't be good for her to hold Charlie now.

"Thanks!"

Michael put a glass of water on the night table and covered Emma with a quilt at the bed's foot. "You rest, and we will be fine!"

Emma was grateful to close her eyes. Michael quietly left the room and bounced Charlie up high as he stepped into the hallway, trying to distract her.

"Well, it looks like you are stuck with me," he said, patting her back. He had never taken care of a child this young. But he didn't have a choice. When he entered the kitchen, he put her in the highchair and asked her what she wanted as a snack. "What about a beer? Well, maybe not!"

He put some juice in the sippy cup and some Cheerios on the chair's tray. She seemed to love both. "We are off to a great start. Hope this lasts so your mommy can sleep." Michael looked closely at the little girl while Charlie was stuffing cereal into her mouth. "You don't look like your mommy. I wonder if you take after your daddy." Charlie wasn't paying any attention to him but loved her snack. That lasted about five minutes, and then she wanted up.

Michael had never had experience with a baby girl. First, he briefly stared at her. Then, he decided she would cry and wake her mother if he didn't get her out of the chair.

"Well, let's play with some of your toys," he said, picking her up and walking into the living room where Emma had put all her toys the night before. He sat her down next to the basket, and she immediately started throwing all of them out! Once the basket was empty, she decided to crawl around the room, ignoring her toys. "Well, that lasted two seconds."

His main concern was letting Emma sleep without worrying about Charlie. "Charlie," he said, trying to get her attention. She decided she wanted to crawl on Michael, who good-naturedly let her do it. His bruises were not too sensitive, so a little thing like Charlie wouldn't hurt him, but he turned to his side so she could crawl better. He would do anything to keep her quiet. Michael vaguely remembered a childhood game of peek-a-boo. He started that game, and apparently, Charlie thought he was the funniest guy ever. They played that for some time.

When that game ended, Charlie wanted to crawl around and inspect pretty much everything in all the rooms. Michael followed around like a servant and picked up objects she shouldn't touch. He was exhausted and tense keeping her occupied. All of a sudden, he thought he smelled something rotten. It was coming from this beautiful child. "Oh no, it looks as if I will have to change your diaper." He headed upstairs to the chest of drawers, which Emma had turned into a changing table. All the supplies were right there. Michael hoped he could figure it out.

Charlie thought it was a big joke that Michael was trying to get the diaper off, so she decided to turn it over several times. The diaper slid all over the place, which was not a good thing with a soiled diaper. He finally remembered how Ella Rose had recommended he could hold her down gently on her chest while he pulled the diaper off with his other hand. Michael grabbed a clean diaper and changed her, figuring out that the sticky tape on either side could adjust to her size. "Clever design, I think!" he said to Charlie, who was watching him intently. Michael put the dirty diaper in the pail next to the chest and rubbed his hands on the disinfected wipes Emma had on the shelf.

"Your mommy is one organized lady," he said to Charlie, who was starting to suck her thumb. "I didn't know kids still sucked their thumbs!" Michael said, picking her up.

She nestled her head into Michael's neck and made a satisfying sound, so he sat in the old rocker Emma had found in the basement. Michael remembered it from his childhood. His mother gave it to him when he bought this house. He was hoping Charlie would fall asleep for a bit of nap. He was exhausted!

After a few minutes, she fell asleep in his arms. He kept rocking, feeling a sense of peace he hadn't felt in a long time. He wondered if she would stay asleep if he put her down in her crib.

He quietly got up to put Charlie in the crib. He laid her down on her back. Tiptoeing out, he hoped she wouldn't wake up. He closed the door but left it ajar. He needed to check in on Emma in case she had gotten worse.

As he went into Emma's room, she turned toward him and asked for water. She had finished the water he had given her earlier. Michael put his hand on her forehead and thought she was boiling. Her face even looked red in the shadows of the hall light. "I'll be right back with water and more aspirin."

Emma ached all over, and her head felt like it would explode. I can't be sick. "Charlie needs me," she thought to herself. She tried to sit up, but her head made her flop back down.

Michael handed her the glass and the aspirin, which she flipped into her mouth quickly. He had to help her get the drink to her mouth as she was shaking.

"Michael, I am sorry. I usually don't get sick," she said, looking up at him. "Where is Charlie?" she asked.

"All tucked into her crib. We had a great discussion about the Chief football game, but then she fell asleep. I guess I was too boring. Do you think you could eat some chicken noodle soup? Mom always gave it to us as kids when we were sick."

"Maybe a little later. I will try to sleep some more and get rid of this headache."

"You sleep, and I will keep an eye on Little Bits."

Emma smiled, thinking about how her perception of Michael had changed in just a few days. He put the quilt over her shoulder as she nestled down into the pillow, feeling sleepier. She slept through the entire night.

CHAPTER TWENTY-THREE

...in which Emma faints and gets a wake-up kiss

E mma woke up and thought she smelled bacon. She sat up and blinked to see if her headache was still there. It was, but standing up made her feel better. She was still a little dizzy. She washed her face and touched her head before slowly heading downstairs. Her head still felt warm. Michael must have picked up Charlie earlier.

Emma peeked in the kitchen and saw Charlie in her highchair, putting Cheerios into her mouth while Michael stood barefoot in front of the stove frying bacon. Emma felt hungry, but she enjoyed the charming scene too much to interrupt it. "Good morning!" Emma patted Charlie on the head but didn't want to kiss her because she could still be sick the night before. Nevertheless, she was surprised that she had slept through the night.

Michael turned around, surprised to see her up and looking much better. "How are you?" he asked while putting his hand on her forehead. "You are still a little warm. I'll get you more aspirin." When had they gotten so comfortable with each other?

"Are you hungry?"

"I am! Maybe some scrambled eggs."

She sat down and gratefully let him serve her some toast. "Could Charlie have some eggs also?" he aske

"Sure! She doesn't know how to use a spoon yet, but give her one anyway. She can pick up little pieces of egg. She likes to put them on a spoon, but it flips over. So she is still learning."

Charlie seemed happy as a lark picking up scrambled eggs with her fingers and putting them onto the spoon. Both Emma and Michael laughed at her attempts.

As Emma sat there, she started to feel a little light-headed, and then the dizziness became worse. "Michael, I don't mean to be more trouble, but I think I'm going to faint." She held onto the edge of the table, trying not to fall onto the floor.

"Whoa," Michael said as he rushed over to the table's side, picking her up as if she weighed no more than a sack of potatoes. He took her to the living room sofa rather than back upstairs, not wanting to leave Charlie alone. Michael took a long look at her face, hoping she would look better. He was worried that the snow had not stopped all night. Fortunately, they still had electricity. As Michael pushed her hair back off her face, he felt a slight tug on his heart. He didn't know much about her, but he did feel she was brave being alone with a baby, probably far away from her home. He figured she had a secret and didn't want anyone to figure it out.

Michael went back into the kitchen and picked up Charlie, who had fallen asleep in her highchair. He put her down on the floor in the living room on a quilt so Michael could keep watch on both of them. It was apparent that Emma's temperature was too high. He gently put a cold cloth on her forehead.

"Well, my mysterious little housekeeper, let's see if a kiss wakes you up!" He gently kissed her cheek and smiled at her sleeping face. Her eyes fluttered up just as he pulled away.

"What happened? Why am I on the couch? Where is Charlie?" she asked as she tried to sit up.

"Hold on, Emma, you fainted. I suspect your temperature is still too high."

Emma put her hand to her forehead and felt the cold cloth. "I have a little headache, but when I woke up his morning, I felt better. Is Charlie okay?" she said, looking toward the kitchen.

"Yes, she is napping right here on the floor. It is warm enough with the fire still burning."

Emma fell back into the pillow behind her head. She was relieved that someone was taking care of her for once. It had been a long time since she had been around people who felt like family. Her eyes closed, and she relaxed on the couch. Emma awoke to the darkened living room, but the fireplace was still burning brightly. She sat up, feeling cooler with no headache. Emma heard voices from the kitchen. Strange how this house quickly had felt like a home, she thought, as she headed to the kitchen.

"Well, hello, sleepyhead," said Olivia, taking off her coat and boots.

"Has the snow finally stopped?" Emma asked, looking over at Michael, who held Charlie as he rinsed some dishes in the sink. She almost laughed at the sight of the big man with a baby nestled in his arms. A shiver went through her at the thought of having to tell him the truth.

"It stopped early this morning, and the snowplows came through right away. This town has always had good snow removal. So what do you both think about a cup of hot cocoa? This kind of weather always makes me think of it," Olivia said without taking a breath.

"Sounds good. I must be better because I am hungry. Can we make pancakes?"

Michael smiled and handed Charlie to his mother. "Not sure you should hold Charlie until your temperature comes down. Pancakes are coming up. I am an expert in the family."

Emma and Charlie loved the positive experience of being so far from home.

These scenes made Emma think of her mom and dad sitting in their kitchen, maybe making pancakes. The memory caught her off guard as she had willed herself not to think of what she left behind for Charlie's sake. But, thank goodness, Phillip couldn't find them, at least not now.

"Emma, are you okay? You looked deep in thought for a bit," Michael asked as he looked over his shoulder.

"Yes," Emma said with a smile. Charlie patted her cheek, and they all laughed. "I think I might need one more nap later, though."

Olivia opened the back door to head back home and looked back at the scene in the kitchen. She smiled to herself before closing the door.

CHaPTer TwenTY-Four

...in which Emma learns how to quilt
and makes friends with a thimble

The next day, Emma seemed much better and appreciated that she and
Michael were growing comfortable. "My temperature is gone," she
said. Emma was tired from her brief illness, but she thought she could work
on the church quilt. "Olivia offered to watch Charlie while I am at church."

Michael nodded and thought she would be okay going out. "I will see
you later. I am waiting for a call from the doctor's office. His nurse thought
I was anxious about the test results, so she said she would call me even on
a Sunday if they came in."

Emma nodded and organized Charlie's bag for a few hours at Olivia's.
Then, after breakfast, she left for the church, taking Charlie to Olivia's,
where they were working at home on some projects for the festival. Emma
wanted to remember to mention the quilt pattern to John. He might enjoy
meeting some of the women who came to the church. She thought it might
do him good to make friends with some women. Her grandmother always
used to say, "It's not over until it's over."

Emma enjoyed learning how to quilt with the very short needles and
using a thimble. That was harder than anything. The best part was hearing
the women sitting around the frame talking about their families and life
in Hill Brook. The quilt was beautiful, and the pattern reminded her of

whirligigs. She wondered if John had seen the quilt. He might be pleased to see the parallels between the quilt and his unique creations.

As she walked into the church basement, she noticed the large frame with the quilt pinned tightly on all four corners.

"Esther Marie, this quilt is beautiful. Who organizes the raffle, and when do the raffle tickets go on sale?"

"They are printing them in the church office this afternoon. They should be ready to hand out for sale this afternoon. Do you want to sell some?"

"Sure, I feel rather proud of being part of this project. I love the Christmas theme of the fabric. The greens and reds are warm and festive."

"Thanks, Emma! We need to sell a lot of tickets."

"Where do the profits go?"

"We support food pantries and community lunch groups. The profits go to fund them. Their clients are mostly working poor in the community, who cannot make ends meet on their salaries."

"That's a worthy cause," Emma responded.

"I think the whirligig booth will support Habitat for Humanity."

"That's great."

There was a commotion in the hallway, and several teenagers came into the room.

"Hi Ms. Morrison, where is Charlie?"

"Hi, Ella Rose. Olivia and Millie are watching her this afternoon. What are you up to today?"

"We are helping with the Christmas Eve pageant. I made lots of new friends at school. I met Maggie Hoxie, who was nice on my first day. Now I know all her friends. She is planning on joining our writing club next week. I think you met her grandmother. I know I am rambling, but I love being here, and the school is so much smaller. The costumes are a mess, and we are in charge of organizing them. You should see the sheep costumes with silver bells tied on with pink ribbons. Hope you can come to the pageant!"

Emma laughed because Ella Rose had hardly taken a breath. "I hope I can go. Charlie might like it, too."

Emma smiled as the girls ran off to the costume closet. She was happy that Ella Rose had made friends in Hill Brook.

"What a cute girl," Mary Margaret said, watching her leave. "She was sweet on Thanksgiving with all of us older folks. She even complimented us on our matching patchwork skirts. Usually, teenagers don't notice anything about older people."

Emma chuckled, thinking about these two women involved in the community. She admired them.

"I better get going to see if Millie and Olivia survived their morning with Charlie," Emma said as she put the needle back into the edging. The women had given her lots of help, and she enjoyed quilting. Learning how to use a thimble was another problem. It kept falling off her finger, but she needed it. The needle would poke her finger without it. Also, she didn't want blood from her finger on the quilt.

Emma was feeling nervous as she headed back to pick up Charlie. She couldn't believe she went back through the alleys behind the houses. Something was comforting to being off the main street. I am paranoid, she thought to herself.

She knocked on Millie's back door and was surprised when Michael opened the door, holding Charlie touching his nose. "Well, hello, you two. Real buddies, I see. So how did you end up with Charlie? Where are Millie and Olivia?"

"I came over to see Mom after the doctor called with my blood tests. It seems I am a little anemic, but everything else is okay." Michael didn't mention the bruises, as he didn't want his mother to find out right now. "Charlie remembered all about our great conversation and peek-a-boo game the other day, so she crawled right over to me. Mom and Millie decided to run to the store for something. I said I would watch her. I hope that was okay."

"Sure. You have developed quite a relationship."

"We have indeed, Emma. Would you like coffee?"

"Sure, I had an exhausting morning quilting my fingers to the bone," Emma said, laughing.

"Well, that deserves at least a cup of coffee."

Michael handed Charlie to Emma while Michael poured a coffee for each of them. "I already gave Charlie a little juice earlier that Mom left. So they should be back soon."

Emma hesitated but said, "Glad to hear about your doctor's visit."

Michael looked away briefly but said, "The other day, the nurse drew a few blood samples but said my blood pressure was good. The doctor didn't think there was anything wrong with my health. Instead, he encouraged me to eat foods with iron. He thought maybe there was something on my mind."

"Well, what are you going to do about it?" Emma asked.

"Not sure. Still don't want to talk about it."

"Fair enough."

"Michael, I just realized I need a pediatrician for Charlie in Hill Brook. She is not walking as I thought she would at her age. I also might let her see a dentist as she has a couple of little teeth. My sister and I didn't go to the dentist until we were older, which scared us. But, we could get her started right away with brushing, so it becomes a habit when older. What do you think?"

"I know a dentist in town, Dr. John Vogl. When we were older than Charlie, he was our dentist, so I am not sure he sees little children. He is a fun guy. His office is next to the yogurt shop downtown. He loves Halloween, dresses up in a costume, and gives out cute toothbrushes. The kids laugh and think he is funny. I am not sure about a pediatrician, but we can ask around."

"Thanks, Michael, great idea."

"Hello," called Olivia as she and Millie came in through the front door. "Hi Emma, I hope you didn't mind Michael keeping Charlie while we ran to the market."

"Not at all. Michael and Charlie were in good form when I got back."

"We picked up a roasted chicken from Molly's and a few sides. Why don't you three stay for lunch? So we can find something that Charlie can eat. She doesn't seem too fussy."

"That sounds great," Emma said. "I think I will change her. Do you mind if I use your room?"

"No, I don't mind at all. Let's eat in the kitchen. We will put lunch on in a jiffy."

The five of them had a pleasant conversation, although no one spoke of the two elephants in the room- what happened to Michael while he was gone and Emma's mysterious background. Instead, they enjoyed Charlie's smiles, and she loved everyone's attention.

After lunch, Emma noticed Charlie was getting sleepy, so she said she would take her back to the house for a nap. However, Michael decided to help clean up the kitchen with his mother and Millie.

As soon as the front door closed and they could see Emma walking toward the sidewalk, Olivia turned to her son and said, "There has been a black sedan cruising slowly around the block a couple of times the past few days."

Millie added, "A man knocked on my front door two days ago asking if I had a guest with a baby staying here recently. I told him that I never share my guest's information with anyone. He left without a word, and I could not see what kind of car he was driving."

"We are worried about Emma but have hesitated to ask her about her situation. We figured it was desperate since she arrived one night with a baby."

"She wouldn't tell me her problems, either, but I haven't been willing to share mine," he said, leaning against the counter.

"Well, we need to keep an eye out and protect the two of them. I doubt she has done anything wrong, but she is too scared to tell us about the situation."

"Maybe I can get her to talk with me tonight," Michael added, putting down the dishtowel and heading to the door. "Thanks for lunch, Mom."

Michael let himself into his house by the front door and could hear Emma whispering to Charlie. He sat down on the couch and waited for Emma to come back downstairs. Within a few minutes, Michael fell asleep himself and didn't wake up for a couple of hours. He figured that Emma had fallen asleep herself, and there would be no heartfelt discussion that day. He peeked in to see Emma and Charlie on his way to his bedroom. They were sound asleep. Emma was still in her clothes. Michael pulled an afghan off the end of the bed and put it over her.

CHAPTER TWENTY-FIVE

…in which John recruits a whirligig work crew

Later that afternoon, Michael decided to go back downstairs. They both needed to face facts about their lives. He brewed a pot of coffee when there was a knock on the door.

"Hi, Mom, what brings you over this afternoon? We all enjoyed the lunch."

"John just called. Walter and Monroe are going back to the wood-working shop in his basement. He wondered if you and Emma would like to learn how to make whirligigs. I could watch Charlie this afternoon at the church. She might like the church nursery for a few hours. After Sunday afternoon devotions, we are helping to sew the binding on the raffle quilt. Everyone enjoys having her there."

"Emma hasn't come back downstairs, but I will ask her. We can bring Charlie over to Hibiscus a little later. Did John say when he would start?"

"I think they are there now. Walter and Monroe have been learning how to do it. They couldn't wait to get back to it today. They even bought new aprons so their clothes wouldn't get paint on them."

"I will give you a call as soon as I ask Emma about it."

"Okay, thanks, Michael."

"Was that your mom?" asked Emma as she walked through the kitchen door, holding Charlie.

"It was. Mom had good news. Walter and Monroe are getting a kick out of working with John and returning this afternoon. They needed a project to work on, I think. I heard it was your idea to get them involved."

"When I met them at the B and B, they only had their morning and afternoon walks to keep them active. So I thought this might help them and John, who is still getting used to being alone."

"John called Mom and suggested we might like to go over to help today. She offers to watch Charlie at the church while they finish the raffle quilt. What do you think?"

"It sounds great. Do you feel up to it?" Emma asked, looking at Michael, thinking that he did look better. The black circles under his eyes were fading.

"I would like to see the process. But, on the other hand, I do want to fool around with tools."

"Could Charlie stay with you while I change clothes? She can sit in the highchair. She might like a little cookie."

"Okay!"

"I will be right back," Emma said as she turned toward the door.

After dropping Charlie off at the church with Millie and Olivia, they walked to John's house. As they walked up to the basement door, they saw Ella Rose running over from her grandparents' home. "Hey, wait for me. I am going to learn how to make whirligigs also."

Emma hugged her and said, "This is getting to be quite the experience. Are you sure you want to spend your Sunday afternoon with all of us older folks?" She looked at Michael and winked.

"You guys aren't old! But, I do like being around adults. Bet we can learn a lot from Mr. Evans."

"Hello, whirligig makers," Ella Rose called as they opened the basement door.

"Hi," said John, who had a small jigsaw in his hand. "You're just in time to help with the sanding. We are trying to finish thirty more before the festival.

Monroe and Morris nodded and waved at them but went right back to painting.

"I cut out the patterns here, and then we move them to this workbench. Then we dust them off and put them over there behind the partition so we don't paint sawdust into the wood. I have an exhaust system that helps. Some people like to wear masks when they are sanding. It is up to you."

Olive Coleman came over mid-afternoon to bring them hot chocolate and scones. "Millie told me you all were over here working hard, so I thought I would bring you a treat," she said. Olive raved about the pieces and how beautiful the finished product would be. She heard about the beautiful quilt that would be at the festival. John was thrilled; it was a similar design to the whirligigs. Emma noticed he kept looking at Olive while sipping the hot chocolate. They were about the same age. They could be a great couple.

After a few hours, Michael and Emma decided to pick up Charlie but assured John they would return sometime that week to work again. Ella Rose met some friends to go to a movie, so she also left.

"See you, Emma. Will you be at the next writing club at Paige Turner tomorrow? John is stopping by to show us how he makes whirligigs and the story behind it."

"I will be there with or without Charlie."

"She was good the last time," Ella Rose assured Emma.

Michael said to Emma, "That was a fun afternoon just working with our hands. I am glad that John thought to invite us both. What was that about a writing club? I knew Elizabeth Turner had been thinking of opening a bookstore in town but so glad it happened."

"The writing club is writing personal narratives, any topic of our choice. I got the idea when I thought about John and remembered Writer's

Workshop in middle school. Our stories start somewhere, and John might share how he started making whirligigs. Then, I thought about writing our own stories and wondered if Ella Rose would be interested. She had just enrolled in middle school here, and it gave her a way to meet people." Emma briefly told Michael how the writing club was going and the funny name.

"It's strange that I had never heard about whirligigs before coming back to Hill Brook. I have noticed them all around town, and now I hear about them every day. They do make me smile," Michael admitted. "I would like to hear John's story about how he got involved. I assume he has a book on how to make them. They look tricky with the special wire attached to the propellers. It's funny that when you focus on a project like that, you tend to leave concerns behind, at least for a bit."

"I agree. Working with your hands can be helpful. I would be interested to know if woodworking had helped John with his grief when his wife died. Maybe he will share his thoughts when he visits the writing club. I think writing down our memories helps us to deal with our current lives."

"Interesting thought. Have you been writing about your life?" Michael asked her.

"I have," she said but hesitated to be specific for fear it would lead to more questions.

He wisely kept silent and didn't pursue it further. "I might have to join your Pencil Pushers one day. When is the next meeting?"

"Tomorrow after school."

"I think I will come to the next writing club if that is okay."

"Sure, that would be great. I hope that we have another chance to help make whirligigs for the festival."

"Me too," Michael agreed.

"The writing club meets after school on Mondays around 3:30 pm at the bookstore. I have made treats, or we buy cookies. Elizabeth makes hot chocolate. We have fun just talking before we officially begin. Since next

Monday is Christmas Eve, we decided to meet on Wednesday after school. It is their last day of school before the holiday break."

"I will buy the cookies for the Wednesday writing session and find a journal I could use."

"Perfect. I think Elizabeth may have an extra one."

After picking up Charlie from the church, they headed back to Michael's house, and Emma went upstairs to put the sleeping child in her crib.

Emma asked, "If you don't mind listening to Charlie during her nap, I would like to go back to the church. I won't be too long working on the quilt this evening."

"Sure, I would like that. I might just read in Charlie's room. That rocking chair is comfortable. Mom told me that it was in my room when I was a child."

Emma put on her coat. She left through the front door but took a minute to look back at Michael, who was walking up the stairs to Charlie's room.

CHAPTER TWENTY-SIX

...in which a hike provides fresh air
and leads to understanding

That Sunday evening quickly passed because Emma learned how to thread a needle, keep the thimble on her finger, and not poke them with the needle.

She headed back to his house after quilting for a couple of hours. Michael had built a fire and was sitting in a comfortable chair with Charlie, reading a story from a picture book. Emma thought it was a lovely scene. She went into the kitchen to get out dessert and coffee.

Michael and Charlie came into the kitchen to see what Emma was doing. "I just read this picture book out loud to her four times," Michael said, laughing. He put the book on the counter and put Charlie in her highchair.

"I read through Time magazine while Charlie slept. I haven't seen a magazine for some time."

Both Emma and Michael were looking forward to attending the next writing club, so Emma played quietly with Charlie while Michael caught up on world news.

"It might be fun to go on a hike tomorrow. There are great hiking trails around here. I haven't felt like talking much, but I could use some exercise."

"Could Charlie go with us?" Emma asked.

"Sure, I will check around to see if anyone has a backpack carrier so that I could put her in on my back.

"I used to have a hiking stick and a safari hat I wore when my sister and I went on a hike in the woods near our house."

Michael wisely didn't ask any questions but wondered about her late-night trip to Hill Brook.

"Let me see if there's enough in the refrigerator to make sandwiches and other munchies. I think I saw a thermos in the pantry for drinks."

"Good idea. I will call around to find a backpack carrier."

"It sounds like fun. What time should we leave?"

"Might be good to leave early in the morning."

"We could stop by Coffee Cafe for coffee and a donut before we leave," Emma added.

"Sure! Just walking in the woods sounds good to me. Have a good night's sleep, you two."

The following day broke bright and clear, but temperatures were moderate for mid-December. Emma dressed Charlie with several layers of clothes and put on a new stocking cap she bought at the boutique downtown.

"Look who is ready to hike?" said Michael as they came down the stairs.

"I think layers might be good as the temperatures might warm up."

"I agree; I did the same thing"... showing his several shirts and jackets.

"Let's head to Coffee Cafe and get a donut. Has Charlie ever had a donut?"

"No, but this would be a great time to try!"

"John had a back carrier he had used for his grandkids years ago. So I just dusted it off, and we are in business."

The cafe was busy, but they found a small table. Charlie loved her glazed donut and munched happily.

"Look who is happy," Michael said, laughing at the sugar all over her face.

He turned back to Emma, who had chosen a stuffed donut and had jelly on her mouth. Michael rubbed it off with his thumb.

"You can't talk; you have chocolate all over your mouth, Michael," Emma teased. "Thanks for the treat. I have enough sugar in me to hike a few miles. Do you have an idea about where to go?" Emma asked.

"I do," he answered. Michael drove a short way out of town to a wilderness area. It looked a little hilly, but no brook visible anywhere. She didn't ask about a stream as they put the carrier on Michael's back and slipped Charlie into it. She wasn't sure how far away the Missouri River was from Hill Brook.

She grabbed the backpack with a blanket and their lunch, then put it on her back. It wouldn't be hard to maneuver and walk.

The path was narrow but walkable. Charlie could hear birds around and kept looking for them in the trees.

Michael was quiet, walking ahead of her. He walked slow enough to match her stride. She had always wished she were taller and had longer legs.

The sun came out, and already Emma thought she might take off her top jacket and tie it around her waist.

They walked silently for about 30 minutes, and Michael turned to Emma and said,

"I could use a drink of water. You put cold water and ice into that thermos this morning, I think."

"I did. Let me get it out of the backpack."

"Let's take Charlie out of the carrier and let her sit on a rock. It might be a new experience."

Charlie sat on a boulder near the path while Emma took off her hoodie and hat while they sat in the sun.

"It is beautiful out here. Who owns this property?" Emma asked as she gazed into the valley below.

"I think this is county-owned as a public hiking area. If I remember correctly, there is a picnic area not too far. Should we try for it?"

"Sure! The path hasn't been a hard hike, and the scenery is beautiful."

Michael picked up Charlie, who played in the dirt around the rock. She grinned at him with dirty hands.

"Let me wipe her hands off first. I do love that she had a chance to get dirty."

Michael settled her in his arms, and they took off for their next stop.

The picnic area came in view quickly, overlooking a pretty valley. Emma looked down, searching for the brook, and no water was visible.

Emma turned to Michael, who spread the blanket so Charlie could sit on it and said, "Is there a brook in Hill Brook? I have been wondering that since I moved here!"

"I have never thought about it. I don't think so."

"It is funny how things get named."

"You're right."

Emma had packed a wonderful lunch of sandwiches for her and Michael. She made small PBJ sandwiches for Charlie. The cold water in the thermos was a refreshing drink.

They sat on the blanket, and both were quiet while Charlie lay her head down on Emma's lap. Her eyes closed, and Michael and Emma lowered their voices.

"The fresh air is good for her. But, winter is coming on fast," Michael said.

"You know, Michael, you look much better than you arrived at the house on Thanksgiving. The dark circles under your eyes are gone, and you look better. Are you feeling better? I know you didn't want your mom to know about the bruises, but are you in any more pain?"

"The bruises are almost all gone. I am not so sore anymore. I still have to deal with what happened, but I'm not ready to share with anyone."

"I understand. Your mom told me you were close to your dad. I am sorry to hear about his death."

"Yeah. Dad was an amazing father. We could talk about anything. But, of course, being an only child, I often spoke to him about my problems. Mom is great, but I tend to protect her from my concerns.

"Both my parents are living. I am close to both of them, although I tend to talk to my mom more."

"Are you an only child?" Michael asked.

"I had a sister who died last year," she answered.

Michael did not question her any further as it felt like intruding.

Charlie sat up and looked around, rubbed her eyes, and tried to stand up. She wobbled a little but put her hand on Michael's knee to push herself up, grinning. Both Emma and Michael laughed at her and clapped for her standing.

"Guess we could head back. It is a downhill hike, so it is easier than coming up."

"I love the exercise, and the day is perfect. Thanks for thinking of the hike."

Michael put Charlie back in the carrier, and they headed down the path. They became quiet and lost in their thoughts.

They noticed Charlie's eyes closing as they arrived at Michael's car.

"Fresh air does make me feel sleepy sometimes, but I feel energized today," Emma admitted.

"I feel better than I have in a long time," Michael responded. "Let's head back to town."

CHaPTer TWeNTY-seven

...in which Emma gets a warning
and Michael has an idea

E mma thought that John might share his story behind learning how to make whirligigs by Monday afternoon. Michael admitted to going to the writing club with Emma on Monday but felt he might not want to write.

"That's okay. You can listen to some of the ideas. These kids are outstanding writers."

As they all settled into the chairs for the writing session, Elizabeth announced that John could not come that afternoon but would come to the next writing club. He had to finish a few whirligigs that needed painting that day. Elizabeth welcomed Michael but didn't ask him any questions.

They started the session with a few people reading a part of what they had written the previous days. Topics prove to be varied and exciting. One student asked if Olive would share what she had written.

"Oh my, are you sure you want to hear my story?"

Everyone was enthusiastic to hear it. "Sure," said Jonathan. "We think you might have the best stories because of all your travels!"

"Well, here goes. One of my favorite, funny memories occurred while living in an Army Quarters in Baumholder, Germany, with my parents while my dad was in the service. We had one of the attic apartments across the hall from a young couple.

One day they asked us to come over to see their Christmas tree. We opened our door, and before we could stop him, our little spaniel, Pete, ran across the hall. He ran over to their tree and peed. We all laughed, but then the wife went to the bathroom to get a towel to wipe it up. She forgot they had attached the tree with a cord leading to the bathroom door so it would stand up straight. When she opened the door to it, the entire tree crashed down. Everyone in the room was startled, and Pete started barking and running around more. Luckily, they laughed, so we could too."

Michael listened to her story and smiled at the antics of her dog. He always loved dogs but hadn't had one since he traveled so much.

"That's just one story I remember. I think dog stories are some of the best. Anyone else has a dog story?" Olive asked.

Several of the teens shared dog stories. Then they spread themselves out in the bookstore to find comfortable places to write. Emma watched Michael write in the journal that they had found for him that afternoon. She wondered what he would be able to write.

As they walked back from the bookstore, Michael walked behind Emma and Olive, who was talking.

Emma said, "Olive, I am so glad I met you at Millie's. Your life must have been interesting and challenging at the same time."

"I am glad too because I often stay by myself in my room at Millie's and don't talk to anyone there. I guess I am so introverted because we traveled so much. It was easier to leave places if I didn't get too attached. Although, of course, there are people who I still write to now and then to keep in touch. It is hard for me to make new friends," Olive admitted.

"I hope you will continue to come to Paige's Pencil Pushers," Emma said, winking.

They were walking down the main street of Hill Brook. Emma kept looking over her shoulder in case she saw the black sedan again.

"Are you okay, Emma? You seem a little nervous."

"No, I am fine," she said, turning around. Emma didn't want others worrying about her. It was puzzling to her that anyone could have figured out how she arrived in this small town in Missouri.

Olive turned away as she walked toward her home, "Bye, Emma, see you at the next writing club. It makes me feel a part of something interesting."

"Me too! See you."

The next day Michael seemed better but still stayed in his room a good part of the day. Emma went to the church to work on crafts for the fair; Michael continued to sleep more than usual, but they ate meals together. Michael seemed to be coming out of his shell. He joined Josh once for dinner at a restaurant, but Emma wasn't sure that he would tell him why he came back early from his assignment. On Monday, he didn't share anything at Writers Club, but she thought he wrote a few things down.

Emma ran into Josh a few times at the hardware store. He was always friendly, never prying. She saw the other police officer several times. He would touch the tip of his cap but never stop to talk to her. She could tell he was suspicious of her, but she always waved and smiled. She would love to set him up on a blind date with Charlotte. Michael might be right that she was a matchmaker.

On Wednesday morning, Emma walked Charlie around the block before freezing again. John waved from his front door.

"Hi Emma, I forgot to mention that I called that number from Kansas City. I let it ring four times, just like you asked."

"Thank you. I appreciate you doing that for me and not asking any questions."

"Are you sure you're okay? We have gotten very fond of you and Lil' Bits," John said as he tickled Charlie under her chin.

"I think I am, but I appreciate that you all are letting me deal with this by myself."

"Well, you need to be careful. Someone was asking about you at Millie's."

Emma's face paled, and she responded with a nod. "Millie told me that she refused to give out any information. I was relieved to hear her say that."

"Listen, Emma; we are all here for you. We will not tell anyone of your presence here. You have been a delight. Whatever is going on, we all think you will tell us when the time is right."

Emma was overwhelmed by his support, so she hugged him. "John, you are a wonderful man."

"That's what my wife was used to say, but it is good to hear you say it. By the way, we are setting up for the festival Friday. It runs from Friday through next Thursday, and then the festivities end on Christmas Eve at the community church Millie and Olivia attend. The proceeds from the sale of the whirligigs are going to the local Habitat for Humanity."

"Isn't that the group that builds houses for people? I think I heard each homeowner needs to spend time helping with the building of the house. President Carter still works on houses at ninety-five years old. That's a great organization to support. What can we do?"

"Are you volunteering Michael without asking him? That's a good sign, my dear."

"Oh, for Pete's sake, he won't mind. I think he will get some professional treatment for whatever is disturbing him. I am not sure if he will be in town that day. I know he wants to be home for Christmas this year."

"I will let everyone know you both will help. I wonder if Michael could help move the whirligigs to the town square Friday. Our booth will be in front of the famous Harley Hardeman's Hill Brook Hardware Store," John said, winking.

"I heard everyone talked him out of using his last name in the store's title," Emma said, laughing.

"I can't resist saying it out loud, to tease him. But, he does run a fine hardware store. He will order the supplies I need anytime."

"By the way, when is the quilt raffle? I had a little part in making it."

"Millie told me you helped cut out fabric and then learned how to quilt when pieced together. I am glad the younger generation is learning to do some of my generation's crafts. My Julie knew how to quilt, but I think she mostly liked to hear the town gossip while the women worked."

"Well, better get home. I feel like I have lived here a long time, rather than just a few weeks," Emma said as she went down his front stairs. She had been lucky to catch John upstairs and not in the basement.

That conversation with John stayed with her overnight. She still wasn't ready to talk with Michael or anyone else, just as he wasn't ready to share what happened to him. Emma remembered a conversation she had had with her father, who had served in the Marines during the Gulf War. He would never talk about things that had happened to him. So, whatever was bothering Michael would take time for him to discuss. It was only natural to resist help. Finally, he told Emma that he had an appointment in St. Louis with a psychologist recommended by the network.

On Wednesday, Emma and Michael left Charlie with Olivia and headed to The Paige Turner for the writing club. Michael carried the box of cookies and his new journal. They met Olive on the way.

"Hello, Michael," said Elizabeth coming over to hug him. "Glad you can join us again. Emma mentioned you had been writing some in your journal."

"I wasn't sure I had any stories in me."

Everyone formed the circle as usual and was chatting happily.

Elizabeth started the discussion with a question about the actual process. "Why would building a whirligig help someone learn anything about life? They were looking forward to hearing why John had started making them. Some thought just physical activity of making something supported people by distracting them from other problems. Maggie Hoxie mentioned that she felt that learning a new skill was helpful. Several kids compared making something to writing thoughts down. They thought writing and creating something could be beneficial when a problem was bothering them.

Michael spoke up, "Like building something," he commented, thinking about John and his whirligigs.

Maggie responded. "Sometimes, when we have trouble, thinking of helping someone else is the answer."

"Wow!" Michael asked, "When did teenagers get so smart? "

They all laughed at his comment. Just then, John walked in with a large bag of wood and hardware. Elizabeth decided they could all stand around one of her long counters and watch how he assembled the whirligigs.

They watched in fascination when he took the wooden pieces and attached the propellers. The curved wire moved the wooden piece up and down. He had brought the mermaid-whirligig, which moved the tail up and down.

"That's complicated," whispered Jenn to Maggie. Neither one of them had ever made anything with their hands.

John shook his head and answered that it was a step-by-step process. "Taking it one step at a time helps me. There is something very comforting about completing each part of the project. Cutting out the pieces is one project. Painting is the next step. Assembling is the final project. It has helped me, I know," John admitted.

Someone asked him why he started making whirligigs. "Well, I have always liked working with my hands. After seeing a few whirligigs at a craft show a few years ago after my wife died, I smiled for the first time in a long while. I changed after that, and getting involved in making these has helped give me a purpose. They seem to make people happy."

Emma noticed that Olive was smiling at the mermaid whirligig and smiling at John's comments. That's the happiest she had ever seen Olive. Everyone seemed surprised at his sharing such a personal thought.

"I think I would like to make one," admitted Michael. "I have a design in mind, but could you help me with it, John?"

"Sure, come on over Friday morning. If you sketch out your design, I will help you cut it out of wood. I guess you heard that Emma volunteered you to help me move all the whirligigs to the display tent. We will be in front of Harley's."

"No problem, I have time in the morning to help."

The group looked at the pieces carefully and talked to John. Finally, some of them wanted to make a whirligig. John said that he would have the time to have them over to the workshop after Christmas. "I wouldn't turn away some sanding and painting help before the festival. We have a few whirligigs to finish by Friday."

When everyone left, Emma turned to Michael. "Does the idea about making the whirligig have something to do with what happened in the Middle East?"

"It does, and I got the idea from what John said. I think I have not been able to think about it rationally. Making a whirligig might help."

CHAPTER TWENTY-EIGHT

...in which a festival kicks off more than just fireworks

Early on Friday, Michael went over to John's workshop. Luckily, John was waiting for Monroe and Walter to finish sanding so he could paint the last few whirligigs.

"What are you thinking about for your whirligig?" asked John.

"I would like to make a man's figure and have it work, so he lifts a video camera to his shoulder somehow. Is there a way to make that work? I am not sure I understand how the propellers and mechanisms work together."

"Why don't you sketch out the man's figure, and I will pull up a photo of a large video camera and trace it on wood. Have you ever used a jigsaw before?"

"You may have to guide me on that," Michael admitted with a grin.

Michael spent the morning learning the steps of making a whirligig. Then, he sanded the pieces cut out and painted them. Later, he realized he would have to finish the next day.

"Why don't you come over before 8? I don't have to have my booth set up until after 10. We can put the hardware on it. I do recommend spraying it with an acrylic spray after that."

"Thanks so much for helping me," Michael said, patting John's back.

Later that morning, the festival committee met in the town square to set up the tents. Emma learned that the city council had invested in really sturdy tents for all the craftspeople one year. It was hard to predict bad weather, and the tents would help if they had rain. They even had a way to attach them to special hooks set in concrete.

Charlie was all bundled in a warm jacket with a hood, but Emma wouldn't let her stay out for a long time. Finally, Charlotte McManus from the market's bakery said she would take Charlie during her afternoon break from the store. Charlotte turned out to be a wonderful friend around Emma's age. She had finally shared her dream of being a nurse and had enrolled in a local community college to get electives completed before going into a nursing program. They had a lot in common, as both women hoped to continue their education.

Michael was going to help John take the whirligigs after he finished the one he had designed. He hadn't told anyone the reason he created it. John's crew had reached the goal of preparing thirty to sell. Walter and Monroe had invested many hours helping make the gadgets. Finally, the three of them had decided to set the price at fifty dollars.

The town square was fairyland with the Christmas lights on tents and trees. Emma was surprised to see that several booths had craft products she had never seen before. The festival would open at seven that evening with fireworks and the giant Christmas tree's lighting in the town square. Emma was impressed by the festive look of the town center.

She couldn't resist the display of wooden Santa figures in the hardware store window, so she and Charlie went inside to look at them again. The memories of Christmases at home were overwhelming her once more. She knew it would be painful to spend time away from family this Christmas, but she was grateful for the people she had met in Hill Brook. She especially loved the wooden carved Father Christmas, which reminded her of many in her mother's collection. They were individually carved and carefully painted. She wondered if they were from Germany.

"Hi Emma, are you looking to buy one of my Santa creations?" Harley asked her.

Emma hadn't noticed him in the aisle next to the display. "Oh, hi, Harley. I adore these Santa wooden ornaments. Are they from Germany?"

"The wooden carved ones are from Germany, but the ceramic ones are from a Kansas City company. So I figured we needed some by local artisans as well. One woman in Hill Brook makes the stuffed Santa toys with fleece. They make great toys for children."

"I think I want to buy one of the carved Santa decorations for my mom, who has a great collection."

"Take it over to the counter, and they will check you out. The cashier can even wrap it up for you if you want."

"Thanks, Harley, will do."

She paid for her gift but decided to wrap the present herself. That was half the fun of Christmas gift-giving, as far as Emma was concerned.

When she came out of the store, she saw everyone was busy setting up for the festival.

"What are those clear crystal balls hanging all over the tree? They seem to have something inside," Emma asked Millie, who had come up behind them carrying the quilt wrapped in brown paper.

"Each one of those ornaments contains a slip of paper with someone's name who has died, with a memory about them. Some ornaments have been there since we started the festival years ago. A week before the festival, children from the elementary school hang ornaments every year. They love that the fire department comes to help them at the top of the tree. It's nice to think that we take the time during the holidays to remember people who have died."

"That is such a great tradition. I wonder if I could get one and put it on the tree?" She thought about her sister, but no one asked her whom the ornament would honor. Finally, Olivia went over to the person working on the tree and asked if she could have one for a friend. It touched Emma that she would remember Susie, even so far away.

After she filled out the little card and placed it in the bright plastic ball, she hung the tree's ornament. It sparkled just like the others. She felt closer to her family than she had in a couple of months. When she crossed the street back toward the hardware store, she saw Michael drive up in his SUV and park with the whirligigs. John had driven with him and had already pulled out a massive piece of wood he used to display all the whirligigs. With their striped aprons, Walter and Monroe were waiting to help him unload their work. They seemed proud to be part of the project.

Michael came over to Emma and Charlie and kissed Emma on the cheek, which caused her cheeks to flush. Then, he picked up Charlie and bounced her up and down and kissed her on the cheek, also. "Boy, are we lucky with the weather? It is chilly but not freezing. I've only been home for a few of the years they have done this festival, but weather can be unpredictable."

Charlie raised her arm to pinch Michael's nose. "Ouch, you little devil. I am going to pinch yours," he teased as he gently squeezed hers. She just laughed, and Michael handed her back to Emma.

"I am going to help John, and the guys set up their display boards. John has fashioned a great way to display them by inserting the poles into cut-out holes in the display wood. That will take a short time. Would you like to go to The Coffee Bean and Chicken Café for lunch after doing that?"

"We would like that," Emma admitted hoping Charlie would forgo her morning nap. Emma suspected she would grow out of one of her naps soon.

By then, most of the tents were standing. The crafters had started moving the tables and display cabinets in first—the booth owners brought the items later that afternoon. Again, Emma was impressed by the organization. Everyone seemed to get along. They had started in plenty of time, so no one felt rushed or stressed.

Michael, Emma, and Charlie met for an early lunch a little before noon. The Café was busy with the festival volunteers, proving it was beneficial to the town merchants to have events like the holiday gathering.

"Hello, Mrs. Blanding, how are you holding up with all the business?" asked Michael as she seated them at a window table.

"We would rather be busy than not. I make extra chicken and dumplings, that's for sure. Josh said he would be busy but doubted there would be trouble with the crowd coming in. Last year, the Hill Brook City Council voted to build a two-story parking garage to accommodate tourists near Main Street. That has helped with parking this time of year. Glad to see our government leaders are ahead of our complaints."

Both Michael and Emma laughed at her joke about city governments. "Let me get Charlie a highchair. I will be right back."

"It seems like an eternity ago that I came into the café on that cold, windy night. I was exhausted and hungry. I am glad to know you were here that night; finally," Emma admitted.

Michael looked at the window as if he didn't want to answer, but he turned and admitted, "I wasn't sure what to do, especially whether or not to go home to an empty dark house. So I stayed at a little motel outside of town. I wasn't sure anyone would recognize me if I came to the café for dinner. The waitress was new, so she didn't know me. Mrs. Blanding never came out of the kitchen that night. If she had, I bet she would have called my mother."

"You just needed time," Emma said, gently touching his hand.

Michael looked down at her smaller hand, covering his, and thought that just people caring helps when life takes an ugly turn.

"Here you go, little lady, a chair just for you. What would you two want to order?"

"I can't resist your chicken and dumplings, and I can share with Charlie," Emma volunteered.

"Ditto for me, but I am not going to share with anyone," Michael said, grinning.

Emma looked over at him and realized the circles under his eyes were not as prominent as before.

"What time do the festivities begin tonight? I think I will take Charlie home for her afternoon nap after I help Millie and Olivia display the raffle quilt."

"I think the mayor opens the evening with a short speech, before the lighting of the Memory Tree, and then the fireworks. This afternoon I will stay and help John for a little while, and we can come back together around seven tonight. Will that work?"

"Perfect! I told Millie I could help sell raffle tickets tonight and some on Saturday."

Their chicken and dumplings came, and the three of them started eating. The conversation stopped for a bit. Charlie still liked to put pieces on her spoon and try to get them into her mouth.

After paying the bill, Emma and Charlie went to the quilt booth. Michael found John at his booth. Crafters were working hard preparing their displays.

Later that afternoon at Michael's house, Emma wiped out the refrigerator. She moved some items to the bins to make room for cookies and holiday dinners supplies. She looked up and saw Michael leaning against the doorframe with his arms folded. Emma thought he had been watching her. All she was doing was cleaning.

"Hi, have you all finished with the whirligig booth?"

"We did. A few of the whirligigs were a little heavier than John thought, and we had to reinforce the stands. They are amazing, especially when you see them all together. A little breeze was all that they needed to make them all move."

"That makes me remember the first airplane trip I took with my parents a few years ago to Washington State. We had just left a tour of an enormous dam, and all of a sudden, we saw this huge area in a park that was just whirligigs. They were all moving at different speeds. It was a special place. We never figured out why it was out in that specific place. We all said it was a Serendipity Moment, never to forget."

Later that evening, after their quick dinner of grilled cheese sandwiches, Emma and Charlie played on the living room floor. Michael was listening to their voices. They were planning to leave for the festival soon, but he enjoyed a quiet time there. Michael leaned back onto the sink and folded his arms over his chest. He felt a sense of peace he hadn't felt in a long time since his brief but horrific assignment in Afghanistan. Michael had been avoiding thinking about that since returning to the states. The cable news network encouraged him to get professional help, but he avoided it. Maybe it was time to face up to what had happened.

"Ready to go for the opening of the festival and the fireworks display? Some of the booths will be open for business for a couple of hours."

"Sure. Charlie had a long nap, and she was ready to go. But, I want to take the stroller. She is getting too heavy for me to carry."

"Here, give her to me while you get out the stroller,"Michael.

Emma got the stroller, and they went outside. Emma felt a secure connection with this man even with all their problems. They walked to the main square and were delighted to see a big gathering crowd.

It was a chilly night, clear and cloudless. Emma knew it would get colder fast, so she wouldn't stay late.

"The whirligig booth looks wonderful. I want John to sell them all, but not all tonight," Emma confessed.

"He has only part of them out right now. John will bring more out as they sell."

"Let's look over at the quilt booth. I need to sell some raffle tickets."

"Let's do it," Michael agreed.

"Hi, Olivia, where is Millie?" Emma asked.

"She is walking around selling tickets."

"I can take some also." Emma volunteered.

"Hello, Mom," Michael said as he leaned over to kiss his mother on the cheek.

"Michael, you are looking better."

"Thanks, Mom. I feel better."

"Have you sold a lot of tickets tonight?" Emma asked.

"Quite a few. Are you staying for the fireworks? They will start soon, just after the speech from the mayor. He has promised to keep it short," Olivia laughed while she winked.

Just then, the mayor's voice came over the loudspeakers, and people gathered around to listen. "Welcome to Hill Brook's Famous Holiday Festival. This celebration is our Tenth Anniversary. We are proud to continue the tradition of our Memory Tree. Raise your hand if you have a person remembered on this tree."

Lots of hands went up.

"Let's have our newest resident press the button to light the tree. Then, would Emma Morrison come up here and bring that beautiful baby of hers."

Emma flushed when she heard him say her fake name but headed up the stairs to the stage. She would draw more attention to herself if she refused.

"Are you ready to light the tree?" the mayor asked Emma, who said, "Yes," and took Charlie's small hand to press the button on the crowd's count. "Three, two, one."

The tree was magnificent, and the little clear ornaments sparkled next to the festive string lights. Everyone clapped and remembered the people who were in their thoughts and prayers. But, the best was yet to come. They all waited for the mayor to signal to start the fireworks. Against the dark, cold sky, they were striking and beautiful.

CHaPTer TWeNTY-nine

...in which Emma and Michael share secrets

As they walked home, Emma was glad they had brought the stroller. Charlie was getting heavier and heavier. Emma took Charlie upstairs to change her into pajamas but brought her back downstairs and put her on a blanket. Emma walked over to the couch and sat down next to Michael, putting his arm around her. Charlie sat up and pulled herself up on the coffee table. She took a few steps around but lost her balance and fell. Michael picked her up and put her in the space between him and Emma, who couldn't remember a more incredible night.

It seemed as if the quiet time pleased both of them. Michael put a couple more pieces of wood on the fire. It was nice to keep the fire burning on such a chilly night. Next, Emma and Charlie sat on the couch. Charlie looked as if she was getting sleepy with her thumb in her mouth. Michael sat back down next to them and put his arm around Emma's shoulders. She leaned toward him, which felt very natural and safe.

"I am glad you feel better, although I liked the time I spent with Little Bits. Charlie is sweet and funny. You have done a great job with her. I am assuming you are a single mom," Michael questioned, looking down into her face.

Emma couldn't speak at first but then admitted, "Charlie isn't my daughter, although I sometimes feel like it," she said, not looking at him.

He didn't show any surprise but picked her hand, "Knowing you only for a short time, I think you must have had an excellent reason for coming here," he responded, looking her in the eye.

His comment gave her the courage to look back at him. "I had to run away with her. After my sister, Susie, died, her ex-husband tried to get custody. He came over to my parents' house when I was there, and he threatened me with a gun. I am not sure he would have used it, but I was terrified. Luckily, Charlie was with my parents at the doctor's. Our family didn't want him to get her."

"He doesn't know when I left, and my parents do not know where I am. I have been wondering if he somehow found out. The black car going around the block and the man asking questions has worried me. I keep thinking that I have made a mistake by running away. My dad drove us to Salem, New Jersey, to catch a bus. We felt that it was better."

"Are you going to hide forever?" Michael asked.

"Not sure. I don't know what Philip might do if he found us."

"Did he hurt your sister?"

"Not physically! He had an affair with a friend of Susie's while Susie went through cancer treatment. He had no remorse when he filed for divorce during her illness. It was a shock for all of us. After Charlie's birth, the doctor found a cancerous tumor during a regular checkup with Susie. She took hormone treatments to get pregnant, and they wondered if that had caused it to develop. It was devastating. Susie started treatments immediately. She was disappointed she couldn't nurse her newborn, as it would have been impossible. Although we were hopeful, I have the feeling no treatment could have saved her at that point. Charlie was only a month old when they started the treatments. They were hard for her because she was still recovering from giving birth."

Michael gave her a tissue when he saw a tear roll down her cheek.

"We all tried to help with Charlie. After the first semester, I decided to come back from college to help my family. With Phillip gone, we decided

Susie and Charlie should move in with us. We tried to make her comfortable and have time with Charlie. The treatments didn't seem to stop the tumor. I think Susie knew she wasn't going to get better. She soaked up every minute she could with Charlie. Susie was the bravest person I have ever known. She never spoke against him, but her husband had humiliated her. Phillip never came to visit during her treatments. Ironically, before her wedding, we tried to convince her he wasn't good enough. She was determined to marry him, and I think they were happy for a while."

Emily took a deep breath and said, "Michael, I am sorry that I could not stop talking. It has been hard not to share this with all of you. The last encounter with Phillip was scary. When my parents heard about him threatening me with a gun in his possession, we thought that was the last straw. They almost called the police! They were angrier than I had ever seen them. We thought a judge might give him custody. My parents will never forgive him for his betrayal. Nor will I."

Michael couldn't help himself. He leaned over and kissed her on her mouth, and pulled her close. Charlie squirmed when he did this, and both Emma and Michael laughed.

"Let me put her to bed," Michael offered, standing up.

"She will need her diaper changed," she reminded him.

"I am quite capable after the past few weeks! So you stay here, and I will be right back."

Emma watched him going up the stairs and thought how her impression of him had changed dramatically in the short time they had known each other.

She closed her eyes and leaned back on the couch, her mind reeling with emotions.

Michael came back down the stairs, sat down next to her, and hugged her. He put his chin on top of her head. "You've had a tough time lately, and I guess I didn't make it any easier when I returned early."

Emma laughed and admitted, "You scared the living daylights out of me the night you came storming into the house. After that, I was planning to leave the next day. I didn't know what to do. You cannot imagine how lucky I felt after meeting Millie and your mom that first day in Hill Brook. They were my guardian angels. It was a dream come true. I immediately fell in love with your home right away. Getting ready for Thanksgiving was wonderful, knowing I would spend the day with your mother and neighbors. I almost didn't miss being at home so much."

Michael looked down at her and said, "The next morning, I figured out more to the story. When I realized that my mother, Millie, and their friend, John, had put together that elaborate housekeeping contract, I knew I couldn't kick you out. I was dealing with a problem of my own and felt selfish being mean to you."

They looked at each other, and Michael asked, "Would you trust me with your real last name and where you lived before coming here?"

"Well, I live in a town near Bergen, New Jersey. It is a large town, but we live in a great neighborhood. It is nothing like Hill Brook. Bergen is right across the Hudson River from New York City, so it feels metropolitan. After Susie died, Phillip came to the funeral and wanted to take Charlie. I was terrified he wouldn't take care of her. I worry that I acted too quickly, but he said he planned to take us to court. We were not sure if we had a case. I suspect I have made things worse by taking Charlie. I feel like I have aged five years in the past year alone. I think of all the immature things I was doing before this happened. Illness in a family can do that to the most immature person."

Michael hugged her and was silent.

Emma took a breath and looked at Michael to see his reaction. "My family name is Ingram; my dad is Harry, and my mom's name is Madge. They have had a terrible time, and I suspect I haven't made life easier for them. They do not know where I am."

"So, Morrison is a made-up name? Running away has been a rough time for you, but you haven't called your family since you got here?"

"I called home from the train station here in Hill Brook but only let it ring four times and hung up. That was our agreement before I left. I asked John to call my parents' number, letting it ring four times when he went to Kansas City. He was curious but didn't ask me to explain myself. It was rather a sad night when we left. It happened quickly. Dad drove me to Salem, New Jersey, and dropped me off at the bus station near midnight. Very few people would have been out. I felt like we were in a mystery TV show. It had started to sleet and snow when I was leaving. Luckily the bus station was dark."

Emma felt sad that she had been afraid to contact her parents and afraid that Phillip had ways of tracking her down. "I can't figure out how he found me. I can't give her up to such a horrible person who cares only for himself. He may have hired a private investigator to find me. My parents have temporary custody, and I have a letter saying I have permission to take Charlie on a trip. Not sure that would be helpful, though."

"I heard from Mom and Millie that they saw a black sedan coming slowly down the street, and the driver was asking questions. So maybe things will work out for both you and Charlie," Mike added as he hugged Emma. " I could get you a burner cell phone so that no one can trace it. Would that make a difference?"

"I hadn't thought of that. It would be nice to talk to my parents," Emma spoke wistfully. Then, she turned to face Michael and said, "I guess you don't want to share your issues with me since I have told you everything."

"You know, Emma, I think we have had enough tonight. And I know you are tired. So why don't we talk tomorrow morning again when Charlie takes her nap?"

Emma realized how tired they both were and thought sleep would be good. Then she felt that he needed to get something off his chest. "We need to talk if you feel up to it. Let me brew a pot of coffee."

Michael answered simply with a nod.

After it finished brewing, Emma handed him a mug of coffee and sat down.

He took a sip. "This is good."

Michael sat a while sipping the coffee, then finally turned to her and began speaking,

"Well, I haven't been able, to be honest with anyone, but maybe I need to share with you."

He looked relieved but also troubled, Emma thought. "Anything you can share? I want to help. I know my presence in your home was not what you wanted when you returned. You remember I saw you at the café when I came to town. I thought then that you were a troubled person. I didn't think you noticed anything that night," she admitted.

"No, I was still feeling out of control and could hardly talk to anyone then. But, remember, I mentioned to you that I was staying at a little motel on the outskirts of town."

"I wondered what happened. Your mother thought it had something to do with your partner who videotaped your reports."

"Well, it does. My partner and I were assigned to an Afghanistan unit to show the daily routine of fighting such a foreign war. My partner was Stanley Abernathy, who videotaped all our interviews. We had been working together for years. He was a great guy, younger than me, intelligent, smart, and loved what he did. We both knew the dangers, but you never believe what happens in a war."

"It is hard to discuss, but we went to a small town outside Kabul. A bomb went off, and Stanley died instantly. I was a little farther back and thrown to the ground. I had some bruises and a few suspected internal injuries, but he was just gone. We had just been laughing about a dog we saw begging in the streets, and we each threw him a piece of our sandwiches. One minute we were laughing, and the next minute he was dead. I feel responsible for his being ahead of me."

Emma just nodded but made no comment feeling that he needed to finish.

"The first therapist I met with suggested that I needed to visit his parents before I could process what happened. I am not sure, I wrote them a note after I got back, but I haven't talked to them face to face. Somehow a phone call does not seem right. I'm not sure how they have been dealing with his death. We only met one time. The network executives have been great. They gave me time off to go through therapy. They even found a therapist in St. Louis, so I won't have to go to New York. I probably will still have to discuss my plans with them at some point. I have a few months off from the assignment. I have an appointment in a few days."

"Would you like to visit Stanley's parents? Of course, you could go by yourself. However, it might be easier with someone else with you."

"I think that might be a good idea. Are you sure you will go with me? I want to take the whirligig dedicated to Stanley and put it in their garden or wherever they want. They live in St. Louis. Unfortunately, I could not attend the funeral because the doctors in Germany would not let me come home. They were concerned I might have internal injuries. I was sorry I missed it, but I did send them a letter of sympathy. When do you think we could go? Christmas is in just a week."

"We could probably leave Monday morning if Olivia and Millie could watch Charlie," suggested Emma.

"I still have to finish the whirligig Sunday," remembered Michael.

"I will call Olivia right now, and we can leave after you finish their gift," Emma said, touching his hand.

cHapTer THIrTY

...in which Michael addresses his problems face to face

Olivia was glad to watch Charlie overnight and was thrilled that Michael was starting to deal with his problems. He had never shared with her that he was injured and was still recovering from the bomb. Michael had had a chance later that morning to share what happened to Stanley with his mom. The whirligig Michael built was painted and dried, so they wrapped it carefully and put it in the back of his car.

By the time they packed up Charlie for the overnight, it was afternoon as they started the drive to see Stanley's parents. Michael told Emma he thought the trip would take a little over five hours, getting them into St. Louis too late to call Stanley's parents.

Olivia had called her sister, Beth, who lived in St. Louis, to have a place to stay overnight. Michael remembered her from visits to see the Cardinals play baseball when he was a teenager. He always called her "Auntie Bethie. "She lives in The Bevo Mill area in south St. Louis City, so it wouldn't be hard to locate. A restaurant there has a massive windmill on a turret, which it would be easy to see from a distance." Luckily, the weather was good. It was cold, but there was no ice or snow.

During the trip, Emma kept talking to keep him focused or distracted with other questions. She told him funny stories about her sister when they were growing up. One of her favorite stories was about Susie and her adoration of individual singers. She always loved Cher. She would wrap a dishtowel around her head and flip it back just like Cher would do with her hair.

"Although Susie was three years older than I was, she was always trying to help me. She was a senior in high school when I was a freshman. She was more outgoing than I am. We always joked that she was the extrovert, and I was the introvert." The more Emma talked, the more stories of her sister she remembered. She recalled the family's joke when Susie wanted to name her baby Charlotte and call her Charlie. Their childhood dog's name was Charlie Brown. It didn't bother Susie, but everyone in the family teased her.

"She enjoyed some time with the baby before she got too sick. As I told you, my sister was the bravest person I ever knew. She started the chemo immediately after Charlie's birth. I know how much she wanted that baby, so I can't give her up to Phillip. He never came to see either Susie or the baby during treatment. He was living with his girlfriend the entire time."

"I understand why you thought it would be wise to leave when you did. Philip sounds threatening."

As they got closer to Columbia, Missouri, Michael said, "Stanley got his journalism degree at Mizzou. He liked everything about reporting but especially the videography and still photography. Stanley took great black and white photographs in Afghanistan. He was young than me, but I met him at an alumni reception at the university when he received special recognition. I graduated from journalism school several years earlier and tried to keep in touch with my professors. Stanley and I hit it off right away, and I recommended him to the network after he graduated."

Emma started asking him more questions about his partner and cameraman. "What was he like?"

"He was a great guy, always professional. He could also be entertaining and witty. He took the best videos, even under the worst conditions. I consider him braver than I could ever be. We were a good team. Not sure how I can ever go back in the field without him."

"I remember the night you had a nightmare a few weeks ago. Were you dreaming about the explosion? "

"Living the moment over and over is a form of PTSD. It won't get better until you deal with it. I've heard about survivor guilt. I keep asking myself why it was him and not me?"

"I am guessing that is a frequent question from someone who survives a tragedy."

"Yes, I think it is. I can't move on until I figure out how to handle Stanley's death. Could I have prevented it? I keep asking myself over and over."

Emma leaned over, put her hand on his arm, and said, "Consider that this is the first step in making things better."

Michael turned to look at Emma and smiled. He was nervous inside, but he felt better having Emma with him.

"It isn't too much farther to my aunt's home. I will wait until tomorrow morning to call the Abernathys."

It wasn't too long before Emma said she saw the Bevo Mill windmill. It was a unique look for a restaurant.

"Her home is just down the street nearby," Michael said.

They pulled up to a two-story home with a bright turquoise front door. His aunt had decorated the front porch for Christmas with the same color theme. Emma chuckled when she saw it. "I think your aunt might be a character."

"My cousins and I always looked forward to our visits every summer. She let us get away with everything. I hope she doesn't ask too many questions. I would rather not discuss it right now with anyone else. You are an excellent listener, Emma," he said, turning to look at her briefly.

"Thank you, Michael. That means a lot. I have always been the younger sister and teased that I was spoiled and immature for my age. I went away for my first year of college at Southeast Missouri University in Cape Girardeau. Several of my classmates in my hometown had heard about their teacher program. I left a few weeks before the fall semester was over. Mom and Dad didn't want me to leave school. When I realized how sick Susie was, I decided to go home. Some of my professors gave me credit for my three education classes. I came home the fall after Charlie was born and after Susie had started her treatments. It was a sobering time. We all tried to keep Susie's spirits up because she wanted to enjoy her baby while she could. She knew she was dying before we did. I am not the silly girl I used to be."

"I suspect you were never a silly girl. On the contrary, you seem mature for your age. We are all impressed with the way you are with Charlie."

"She is easy to love, that's for sure. Her mother adored her. I know Charlie will never remember that time. Dad took photos of them together, so I will show them to her and let her know how wonderful her mother was."

"I know you will," Michael said as he patted her hand. Let's go meet the dragon lady."

They walked up to the front door. Michael's aunt must have seen them walking up the sidewalk. She opened the door and welcomed them enthusiastically.

"Michael, come give me a hug…one of your bear hugs," she called.

He hugged her gently as he didn't want to mention his injuries.

"And who is this delightful young lady?"she asked, looking at Emma.

"Aunt Bethie, this is my friend and housekeeper, Emma Morrison. Emma, this is my aunt." He didn't want to say Emma's real name. She had yet to share her story with Olivia and Millie.

"Well, aren't you the cutest gal and a housekeeper to boot? So come on in, and we can have drinks before dinner."

They settled in the large living room with an old brick fireplace and a beautiful bay window. Aunt Beth brought out a tray of appetizers with a bottle of wine. "I bet you two are a little hungry after the drive. That highway has more potholes than Swiss cheese."

They relaxed for a bit as they chatted. Michael's aunt must have heard he was having some issues but didn't bring it up. She had her kitchen table set for just the three of them. Emma always admired older homes with character and charm. She looked around the dining room as they walked through to the kitchen.

They both enjoyed the delicious beef stew. Emma thought she tasted a little sherry in the gravy. After coffee and dessert, Michael's aunt finally asked him a question.

Michael, why did you make this trip? Your mother told me you came back from Afghanistan early, but I didn't know the reason."

"I have shared the story with my mother and Emma, but I will tell you that my partner, Stanley, was killed in an explosion. It has been shocking, and I am devastated that he died."

"Why are you in St. Louis right now?"

"My therapist thought it would be helpful to talk to his parents. They live somewhere near Washington University. I will call them in the morning. Unfortunately, I could not attend his funeral because I was still in Germany."

"Why were you in Germany?"

"I was thrown to the ground and had bruising on my chest. The doctors were afraid I had internal bleeding. It was just a safety measure, and I am on the mend. Aunt Beth, I have not mentioned this to my mother, so could we keep it between us for the time?"

"Of course, you look pretty good after all you have been through."

"I almost couldn't go home. I was so disturbed the therapist thinks I have survivor guilt, which can be debilitating."

"He is much better than when he first came home," Emma said, putting her hand on his arm. "Michael was startled to find a house full of guests for Thanksgiving dinner instead of a calm, quiet home in which to rest. He shocked his mother, who hadn't expected him for a year."

"You have been through a terrible time. Healing and recovery are time-consuming, and most people have difficulty with patience. The hardest virtue, I think," his aunt added.

"Emma has the cutest little girl, Charlie, who doesn't know any of this tragedy. She is a great comfort to me,"he said, winking at Emma, who knew he wouldn't share her secret for the world.

"How old is she?"Aunt Beth asked.

"She is almost fourteen months old and an easy baby. Almost a toddler."

The mantle clock chimed 11, and Emma and Michael realized they were tired.

"Why don't we call it a night? Sleep as late as you want. Then, you can call them late in the morning."

"That's a good idea, Auntie Bethie," he said, winking at Emma. "That's what we used to call her when we visited in the summer."

Emma chuckled that this big man was calling his aunt Auntie Bethie.

"What are you laughing at?" Michael asked as he headed to the stairs.

"I like the name you called your aunt."

"Old habits die hard. My mother's sister will always be Auntie Bethie, but Aunt Beth is fine."

"I have always enjoyed that my nieces and nephews call me that to this day. It makes me feel special. Michael, take the room on the right, your cousin John's old room, and Emma, you can take Annie's old room. It is down the hall on the left. There are two bathrooms upstairs, so take your pick. I am glad that I kept this old house for evenings just like this one."

"Thanks for dinner. It was delicious. I want the recipe for the beef stew. Did I taste a little sherry?" Emma asked.

"You did. I think it gives it a rather elegant taste, don't you?"

"I do. Thanks again."

Michael hugged his aunt, and now she understood why it wasn't his usual bear hug. She watched them head upstairs and thought that these two were cute together. She thought maybe Emma was the one helping him through the crisis as much as the baby was.

CHAPTER THIRTY-ONE

...in which Michael learns to forgive himself

Both Michael and Emma slept a little later than usual. At least Emma felt it was the first night not worrying about Charlie for weeks. She had slept well and felt relieved that Michael was reaching out to the Abernathys. Emma hoped talking to them would help them all.

Emma thought she smelled muffins baking as she went around the corner into the kitchen. Beth is a woman who likes to cook and bake, Emma thought.

Michael came into the kitchen and looked as if he had taken a shower. "That is a great shower, Aunt Bethie. Is it new?"

"Yes, I decided after your uncle died a few years ago, I would stay in this drafty old house. So I upgraded a few of the old features, including the kitchen and the bathrooms."

"Well, it was a great way to start the day. I smell coffee."

"Help yourself; the machine is easy to operate."

The muffins were hot and steaming, and Emma couldn't wait to put the soft butter on them. "Yum," was all she could say.

After they finished their coffee and muffins, Michael left the room to call Stanley's parents. He hoped they would be able to visit them today. Michael had brought along the whirligig made with John's help. If they were in the right frame of mind, he wanted to give it to them to honor their son. Also, his parents might have questions if their son suffered when he died. Michael knew Stanley's remains had been shipped home for burial, but the coffin was not open for obvious reasons.

"They are home and would like to have us come by and have lunch with them. I decided to call Stanley's parents before we left, not surprise them. They were expecting my call. I think they want to talk and ask questions. Is that okay with you?" he asked Emma.

"Of course, I want to support you and the memory of your partner and friend. Let me get my coat, and I will be ready to go."

"Michael, when you finish, why don't you come back here, and I can take you both to the Bevo Mill for dinner? It is German to the core. It's a fun place for beer and fantastic bratwurst."

"I will call my mom to see if she can keep Charlie one more night and ask Emma too. She is probably really missing her."

"Who am I missing?" Emma asked as she walked back into the kitchen

"Auntie Beth is inviting us to dinner. Would you like to stay over one more night? I can call Mom to see if it is okay."

"That sounds fun. I am sure Olivia is taking great care of Little Bits. What did you call her the first morning, a rugrat?" she teased.

"Not my finest moment for sure, but she is in my heart now."

"Take care, you two. I will be praying the visit goes well."

"Thanks for being a great hostess. We will be back later this afternoon," Emma called as they walked down the sidewalk.

It was a quiet drive through the southern part of the city to The Loop, a popular area in St. Louis with all restaurant and entertainment types. Michael explained that the Blueberry Hill Restaurant was famous for its food. Also, Chuck Berry had often performed in the Duck Room before his death.

Michael found the tree-lined street, but it took some time to find a parking spot. They sat in the car, wondering how they would discover Stanley's parents. The funeral must have been a terrible time for them both.

"Here it is on the left with the red door," Michael said.

He waited until Emma came around the car. Then, they walked up the stairs and rang the bell.

"Hello, Michael; Jo is waiting in the living room. She will be pleased you stopped by. She has many questions for you."

"Howard, this is Emma, a friend of mine, Emma; meet Howard Abernathy."

"Pleased to meet you, Emma. Both of you come on into the living room. Jo opened some wine."

"Michael, thank you for coming. I am glad you can stay for lunch. Come sit down," Jo said as she hugged him.

"It is nice to see you," Michael responded. "Jo, this is Emma, a friend of mine."

"May I offer you some wine or maybe beer? St. Louis is a beer town, you remember," she said as she smiled at him.

"Thank you, Jo. "They all sat down.

Michael took a sip from the beer can then set it down. He said to both of the Abernathys, "I am sorry that he died while covering a story in Kabul."

"We have been thinking about him for months now. We realized that he died doing a job he had wanted to do for years. All he could think about in college was getting his degree in journalism with a minor in video production. He loved working with you, and the job made him feel important. He was too young to die, but we have felt it was important for him to fulfill his dream. Honestly, we were always afraid for you both in dangerous assignments."

Michael and Emma could see tears forming in her eyes as she spoke. Mr. Abernathy added, "We were sorry you were not well enough to come for the memorial service. We heard the doctors were not sure if you had internal injuries."

"I had bruising in my abdomen and chest. The doctors weren't sure that's all it was, so the internist kept me for a few extra days."

"We are glad to see you are doing well. We mentioned you at the service because Stanley thought highly of you. However, we do want to ask you if he suffered. We have been worried about that."

"No, it was sudden. The last thing I remember is that we were laughing about something. We had befriended a little lost dog. We had just thrown the skinny creature a bite from our sandwiches for lunch."

"That is a little comforting," Jo said with sadness. "We announced the day of the memorial that we would set up a scholarship at Mizzou in his name for journalism."

"That is a brilliant way to honor him," Michael added. Emma felt comfortable just listening to the conversation.

"What about you, Michael? Are you feeling okay? What about your position with the network?" Mr. Abernathy asked.

"The network is giving me some time off to work through this."

"I hope you are taking advantage of that time to figure out what you want to do," Jo said.

"I have an appointment with the network executives in a few days in New York, but I will be home for Christmas."

"That's good," she responded.

"I have a present for you," Michael said. "I will get it from the car."

Both Jo and Howard looked at each other in surprise.

"I will be right back," Michael said.

Michael brought the whirligig in from the car and got a pole that could be attached. They were surprised and seemed delighted that the figure was a video journalist. He showed them how it would move when the breeze turned the propellers.

"This is wonderful, Michael. I know it took some time and thought to make."

"Where would you like to put it?"

"I think I would like to put it in my rose garden. We appreciate the thought. It looks challenging to make with the propellers creating the wires that turn to make it move."

"I just read a book about a boy who made whirligigs to honor a young woman who had died through an automobile accident that he caused. I think he gained peace, making the apparatus. I think I did, too. I will remember Stanley for the rest of my life."

Michael turned to Howard and asked, "Would you like me to put the pole in your garden? It doesn't need to be seated in concrete, just firmly packed soil."

"That is a great idea. It rained here yesterday, so it should be easy to dig in the ground. I will find you a shovel." The two men left to head to the garden.

"Emma, why don't you help me put lunch on the table. Nothing fancy, just soup and sandwiches," she added. They walked to the kitchen. Jo asked Emma to pour iced tea and put out the sandwiches while heating the soup.

"How did you happen to get the job as Michael's housekeeper?" she couldn't resist asking.

Not willing to share the whole story yet, Emma just said, "Charlie and I ended up in Hill Brook to avoid a difficult situation. Michael's mother figured I could use a place to stay and a job. Taking care of his home was perfect. I had been living there for weeks when he came home unexpectedly. He looked weary and hurt but hid that he was physically not himself. Everyone thought he was suffering mentally, and we tried to let him rest, but eventually, he felt better after talking to a therapist. I think he was feeling guilty that he did not die along with Stanley."

"Oh my, I am sorry. Stanley would never want him to feel like that."

They looked out the bay window looking over the garden where Michael was putting in the whirligig. He was tapping down the soil around the pole. A cold wind came up at about the same time, and the propellers started moving. The video cameraman moved up and down.

"That is wonderful. Stanley would have gotten such a kick out of it. He was his mentor and idol for the years they worked together," Jo said as she touched Emma's shoulder.

Lunch was pleasant for them all. The Abernathys and Michael shared stories about Stanley. It seemed to be cathartic for all three of them. Emma felt included in the feeling.

"Thank you for talking to us today," Michael said as they both stood up. Jo and Howard walked them to the front door, each hugging him. "It was nice to meet you, Emma," Jo said as they shook hands.

"Thank you for lunch. It was perfect. This time has been beneficial for Michael."

After they got into the car, they shared a sigh of relief. Emma turned to Michael and smiled, "Hope this trip was what you expected."

"I didn't know what to expect, but it was better. I will always miss Stanley, but he loved what he did. We knew the dangers of what our jobs entail."

"When do you leave for New York? You said you would be back for Christmas."

"I will do everything I can to be back. I need to check in with the network and figure out how to handle my treatment. I think the executives are considering it PTSD. The therapist I saw once agreed. I'm not sure he will take me on as a client. The nightmares I have been having are also a symptom."

When they got back to his aunt's home, Michael asked, "Would you mind if I tried to see the therapist this afternoon that the network recommended here? I have spoken to him on the phone. I am not sure I can get an appointment, but I would like to plan how to proceed since we are so close."

"Of course not. I will stay here with Beth, and I will give Olivia a call."Emma said.

Michael called the therapist's office to see if they had an opening that afternoon. He was lucky they had a cancellation. He told Emma and his aunt that he would be back in a couple of hours.

"We can head over to Bevo Mill for dinner after you return," his aunt called from the kitchen.

"Thanks," he said as he closed the front door.

As Emma called her now, Beth made a pot of tea. They sat and talked about Michael. Beth told her stories of their extended family getting together for reunions in St. Louis. Two generations before, their ancestors had been immigrants from Germany.

Emma mentioned that her mother had also been interested in family history and researched both sides of their family. She thought it was fun to learn about ancestors and how they came to America. Two hours had passed before realizing they had been talking that long. The sun had set without them noticing.

"Michael should be back soon. I will go and wash up. It has been so nice of you to let us stay here. The trip was stressful for Michael but staying with you was perfect."

Emma went upstairs to change clothes for dinner, as did Beth. Emma wanted to check in with Olivia to see how they managed Charlie. She felt better hearing that Charlie was having a great time. They had spent some time at Millie's, where all the residents had made her the special guest.

Michael came back shortly after they were ready, and they headed to dinner. Neither Beth nor Emma asked him how his appointment went. Instead, Beth drove them to the restaurant in just a few minutes. The windmill turning slowly over the roof impressed them. Constructed of attractive stone, the restaurant had blue shutters. It had an authentic German feel. They decorated the flowers boxes with evergreens and holly with red bows in December, but Emma could picture red geraniums growing in warmer months.

They entered the front door to a large beer hall with long tables and benches. The atmosphere was festive but not too noisy. They found empty seats at the end of a long communal table. All three of them ordered beer and warm, soft pretzels because they were all hungry. The wait staff was friendly and took their order of bratwurst and German Potato salad on the side.

Beth and Michael continued their conversation, reminiscing about their family reunions. Suddenly, a waiter on the other side of the hall dropped a tray with glassware and china. Michael jerked up, almost upending the table. He put his hands on the top of his head, then turned, and hurried outside the restaurant.

Beth said, "Why don't you follow him and see if he needs help."

Emma hurried outside and found Michael squatting against the wall. His head touched his knees. He still had his hands on his head.

"Michael, are you okay?" Emma asked as she knelt.

Michael did not answer back right away. He finally stood up and looked at Emma. "I am sorry. I thought I was back in Afghanistan for a second, and it sounded like a bomb."

"This is a symptom of PTSD, I think. Did you tell your therapist that you have had nightmares as well as reactions like this one?"

"I did mention all my symptoms. I got the impression we would tackle them one by one."

"It could be a long process, you know."

"The therapist was realistic and said it would take time. I am just glad I don't have to travel too far to see him."

After a few minutes, Emma asked, "Are you okay to go back inside?"

"Yes, I am better. My heart was racing before."

Michael apologized to his aunt, who was very supportive and understanding, patting his hand affectionately. "No worries. You will pull through this in time; just take it one day at a time. I think you need to let Emma help you."

Michael looked over at Emma and smiled. "I think I do."

Their meals came, and they were able to enjoy the bratwurst. The evening ended on a sweet note. They all went to bed early so that Michael and Emma could leave promptly in the morning to return to Hill Brook.

CHAPTER THIRTY-TWO

*...in which gingerbread houses make
more holiday memories*

The following day, the trip back to Hill Brook was quiet as they reflected on what had just happened. Emma thought about what she might do to straighten out her own life.

They picked up Charlie, who was sound asleep. When they got to Michael's house, Emma went upstairs to put her to bed.

Michael watched Emma walk up the stairs and thought about handling talking to a professional about what he went through. He had been avoiding dealing with it and taking it out on everyone around him. Maybe it was time to try to work through it. He was glad that he had started to talk to the therapist the day before. They set up a series of appointments in January, making him feel better. He turned out all the lights and checked the doors before going upstairs.

The next morning Emma woke up just minutes before she heard Charlie making noises in her crib. She put on her slippers and peeked in the door watching as Charlie entertained herself playing with her feet. Finally, she peeked over at Emma and stood up, shaking her crib and laughing.

Emma picked her up, marveling over her good nature. She was startled to see they had slept late. It was almost 11. Why hadn't Michael awakened her? She thought she heard some noise from the living room.

They both got dressed in warm clothes and walked downstairs to see what was happening. Emma was surprised to see Michael holding onto a large evergreen tree, trying to stand up straight.

"Let me help you!" she said, putting Charlie on the blanket on the floor. She held the middle of the trunk while he crawled around the bottom to twist the screws on the stand into the tree's trunk.

"Okay, let it go and see if it stands up!"

They held their breath as she let go. It was just right. Simultaneously, Charlie had crawled over to Michael and started pounding on his back as she laughed her unique chuckle. They started laughing. Emma felt a warmth cascade into her whole being.

She had been lonely since she left her home.

Michael turned and grabbed Charlie. He raised her above his head, jiggling her gently.

Emma couldn't help but tear up at the scene. "Thank you for the tree!" she said with bright eyes.

"Emma, I think I will fly out to the headquarters of my network in New York and see what they recommend. I cannot deal with it on my own. I thought I could, but the nightmares and the other night at the restaurant show me I am in trouble."

"I am glad you have shared what happened and talked to Stanley's parents."

"It has made me realize I need more professional help. Knowing you are here watching Charlie and the house also makes me feel better."

"When are you going?" Emma asked, dreading the answer.

"I have a flight out Friday afternoon, but I will get the network's recommendations and return at least by Christmas Eve.

"I am sure this is the right answer for you, but we will miss you," she said as she hugged him. It was a comfortable feeling that she had never felt before.

Charlie crawled over and hugged Michael, but on his leg. Michael laughed as he picked her up, and the three of them stood in the middle of the living room.

"I found several boxes of decorations in the basement that should be enough for the tree and other decorations for the house in the attic. I also found your records and boxes of photographs. I found a picture of you and Stanley taken in a place that didn't look local. I hope you don't mind; I was looking around."

"Of course not. I will have to go up and see some more photographs. I don't want to forget Stanley."

"What about putting lights on the tree today and decorating before you leave for New York on Friday? I suspect Charlie will take off ornaments from the tree's bottom branches as fast as we will put them on. Let's do that. Then I need to get ready for the gingerbread decorating party tomorrow." Emma was looking forward to making gingerbread houses with Ella Rose and her friends the next day.

She was surprised that eight of Ella Rose's friends could come, and each of them would bring a bag of candy. Emma covered Michael's dining room table with butcher paper several layers thick so the sticky candy would not hurt it. She had also bought some candy. Michael surprised her by buying some red licorice whips for making bows and other candies for the decorating. "I am only doing this so I can eat the candy," he admitted with a grin.

Emma had picked up green wreath sugar candies and red and green M and Ms. The icing came with the kit and would harden so the candy would stick to the gingerbread.

On Thursday, Ella Rose and her friends arrived at 4. They were excited about the holiday break from school. Emma put Charlie in her highchair to see all the teens working on their houses. They gave her some mini marshmallows, but they discovered she loved to throw them as much as eat them.

Ella Rose came over to Charlie immediately and gave her a little hug. "You get cuter and cuter, Charlie. Are you going to decorate a house?" Emma was surprised that some of the boys came to make a house. Ella Rose mentioned to them that Michael was decorating one with Emma, giving them the courage to do it. The teens' creativity and imagination impressed both Michael and Emma as they figured out ingenious ways to decorate.

Ella Rose wanted to use small, shredded wheat for the roof with overlapping shingles. Some teens used candy as shingles on other houses. Ella Rose said, "Jonathan, I can tell you want to be an architect because you used caramel squares to brick the entire house. It looks fabulous!"

Maggie used tiny candy canes as a festive doorway. Then, with the fondant, she carefully shaped a whirligig for the yard of her house.

"Oh my, Maggie, your tiny whirligig is amazing." After that, each one of the teens made a fuss over each other's house. Jenn finally said that everyone had to gather around and asked Michael to take a picture of the finished gingerbread houses and the group.

Ella Rose came over and hugged Emma, "Emma, you have made this a special holiday season. I want to live here in Hill Brook. I hope my parents can get home before New Year's. I need to talk them into buying a house here so I can stay at Truman."

"Your grandparents would be thrilled, as we all would be," Emma added.

Michael looked over at Emma when she said that. He wondered if she was thinking about staying in Hill Brook herself.

All the gingerbread houses were so cute. Lined up looked like a quaint village. Michael and Emma worked on one together and laughed when several pieces slid off.

Some of the candy ended up on the floor, but Michael just laughed and got out the broom. Ella Rose and Maggie stayed to help. The brown paper was a brilliant idea because Emma rolled it up and out to the trash it went. She was thrilled with the gingerbread houses. Charlie had had a great time eating and throwing the marshmallows. Emma couldn't resist hugging Michael after cleaning up the candy and said, "What a fun afternoon! Thanks for all your help."

"Maggie, did I hear you are saving up for college already? Aren't you a sophomore in high school?"

"KU. I hope to get a scholarship, also."

"Good for you. I hope to go back to finish my degree in education soon," Emma added as she hugged each as they left.

"Emma, I agree with Ella Rose that you have made this holiday much better than I thought it would be!" exclaimed Michael.

Chapter Thirty-Three

...in which a Labyrinth leads to Hog Heaven

Friday morning, both Michael and Emma went shopping for Christmas gifts. A weight lifted off Michael's shoulders. He wanted Emma to feel the same way but wasn't sure how to make that happen. Later that afternoon, Michael said, "Emma, you might like to see the new Labyrinth that Community Church built last summer. They made it wide enough that wheelchairs could get around. I think that Charlie might get a kick out of it. Her stroller would fit fine, and two people could walk together. They have trees and all kinds of interesting plants."

"What exactly is a labyrinth? I've heard of them but don't think I have ever seen one."

"It is a unique path to help people meditate and feel calm. I am not sure of its history, but the design might be scientific. Each turn in the walk is 180 degrees, and supposedly the mind resets itself. So there can be many turns while walking."

"Do you want to go this afternoon? The weather has improved, and it isn't so chilly right now."

"Let's do it. Maybe we could stop for dinner on the way back. You have been cooking for me long enough. Time for me to cook for you," he said with a grin.

They quickly walked to the church and went around the back. Emma was surprised to see a vast walkway with stones lining it. Just like Michael described, it was elaborate and stunning. Solar lights in the ground turned on as dusk was coming. There was a tree in the middle with a wooden bench. They started through the archway and walked silently up and down, back and forth, without talking too much. It was peaceful. They both seemed to be thinking to themselves. Charlie kept looking from one side to the other and laughing.

When they got to the middle, Michael suggested sitting down. More lights were coming on, as were Christmas lights sparkling in the trees. Emma felt a sense of absolute peace and contentment. She still felt guilty overreacting quickly to Phillip's threats and leaving her home. Yet, she felt that somehow this was all meant to be.

Charlie was tired of being in the stroller, so Michael offered to carry her on the path outside the Labyrinth. Neither one of them spoke until they completed the walk.

Emma spoke first, "That was amazing! I felt something each time I turned the half-circle. I might have to read about the science behind that. Thanks for bringing me here."

"It was a good experience for both of us, I think. The festival is ending tomorrow, so I thought this would be good to do before. What sounds good for dinner? I haven't had a barbeque since I returned. Want to go to Hill Brook Hog Heaven? It is not too far out of town. Unfortunately, we will have to go back to the house to get my car."

"That's fine. I am getting a little hungry."

The trip to Hog Heaven was quick. As crowded as the parking lot looked, there was no waiting line. Charlie was enjoying the outing with Michael as much as Emma. She loved his attention. When they walked in the door, they noticed Josh and Amy were having dinner at one of the booths. However, they didn't interrupt them because they faced away from the front door.

"Let's not bother them," said Emma with a grin.

"They're probably discussing the fundraiser for the library," Michael responded.

"Sure, they are," Emma answered.

After settling and getting Charlie out of her coat, they ordered and asked for crackers to keep Charlie busy.

Since they discovered they both loved ribs, they agreed to share a big order. Emma ordered chicken for Charlie, which she could cut up for her to eat. At the rate of speed, she ate the crackers; she might not be hungry for dinner. It was always a gamble when children would get tired of sitting while adults were still eating.

She lasted for about twenty minutes, then fussed and squirmed in her chair. Just about that time, Josh and Amy came over to say hi.

"How do you like Hill Brook Hog Heaven?" Josh asked Emma.

Wiping the sauce from her mouth, she answered, "Love it. These ribs are amazing! Next time I won't share." She winked at Michael.

Amy noticed Charlie squirming and offered to take her outside and walk around a little while they finished their meal.

"That would be great. Charlie would like the change of scenery, I am sure."

Charlie went right to Amy like they were old friends, and they went outside with her.

"Wow, this was a great idea! I loved the ribs."

"We used to hang out here all the time in high school. Our parents trusted us when we came here. Too many adults around for us to get in trouble."

"Were you a troublemaker, Michael?" she said, joking.

"Not really. My best friend Atticus and I were both. We were pretty serious in our schoolwork, although we did like to prank each other from time to time."

"I would love to hear about your pranks sometime."

"That's for another time; maybe we better go rescue Amy and Josh from Little Bits."

After paying the bill, they headed out to the parking lot to see Josh holding Charlie on his shoulders, marching around. She was laughing and pounding his head.

"Thanks for the help tonight, Amy and Josh. I just had to finish my last rib."

"She is so much fun. Do I have to give her back?" asked Josh.

"I think you might not like her changing her diaper," Emma responded.

"I had younger sisters and brothers, so I have done my fair share," he laughed.

Michael took her off Josh's shoulders and hugged her while Emma put the stroller back in the car.

"How are the plans coming for the library tech fundraising?" Emma asked

Amy answered, "I filed a technology grant, but we are starting planning for a wine tasting on Valentine's weekend. The winery outside town has agreed to host and supply some wine. I think they hope to sell lots of bottles. We all benefit. Do you want to be on the planning team?"

Michael and Emma looked at each other. Emma said she would talk to her later about it. However, neither of them wanted to discuss the future at this point. On the way home, neither Michael nor Emma said anything about the fundraiser planning team because they didn't know where either one of them would be in February.

Michael helped John with the whirligig booth the next day, which opened every evening from seven to nine. The committee decided to end the festival that afternoon. Emma continued selling raffle tickets for the Christmas quilt, which was very popular. The festival ended at noon. The

booths opened every evening for two hours, but they would close soon. John was thrilled that almost all the whirligigs sold.

The announcement of the winner of the Christmas quilt was to be the final event of the festival at noon. The mayor came up to the stage and said, "Drum roll, please! Turn the raffle ticket container several times to mix them up. We have sold a record number of raffle tickets this year, so thanks to everyone in the community."

Two girls from the Girl Scout troop turned the container over several times, and then one girl closed her eyes and picked out a ticket.

"The winner of the Christmas quilt raffle is… Emma Morrison!"

Emma was shocked and stood still. "Emma, you won!" Michael said.

She leaned over and whispered to Michael, "But I didn't buy any tickets for myself. I was so busy selling them." Then she laughed.

Michael took Charlie from Emma's arms and pushed the surprised woman toward the stage to pick up the quilt. Everyone was clapping and cheering as the mayor gave it to her.

Looking at the quilt as they started to walk home, Emma said with tears in her eyes, "It is beautiful. I love it."

Before leaving the festival, Olivia, Millie, Mary Margaret, and Esther Marie all came over and hugged her.

"I am glad you won it!" Esther Marie said.

"Thank you. I will treasure it always," Emma said, wondering who had put her name in for the raffle.

Michael and Emma helped the quilters close up the tent and put away whatever crafts were left.

"The tent committee will be here tomorrow morning to take down the tents to store them for next year," Michael reminded her.

Monroe put the two left in the hardware store to sell another day as they passed John's booth.

"Emma, come over here, please," John called. "Did you know that Olive came over several nights to help us sell whirligigs? She even wore an elf costume and hat. She was so enthusiastic. I had never met her before Thanksgiving. Did you ask her to help us?"

"No, I didn't, but I am so glad. Olive seems to stay by herself a lot, which is a good sign. I am not too sure when her husband died and not sure when she moved to Hill Brook."

"Well, I might ask her out for dinner to pay her back for all her help. What do you think of that?"

"I think you are a wise man," Emma said and hugged him. "Congratulations on selling so many whirligigs. You will need rest."

"I have many orders for spring. After New Year's, we will be back to work."

"Good night, John," Emma said, turning away.

"Bye, everyone," Michael said as they left the town square.

CHAPTER THIRTY-FOUR

*...in which Michael leaves, and Emma
gets an unexpected guest!*

They arrived back at Michael's home just in time to call for a cab to take him to the train station. Charlie fell asleep on the way home, but they put her on a blanket in the living room.

They heard a honk in the driveway. Michael got his satchel by the door. He came over to Emma, hugged her, and kissed her forehead. "I will let you know when I get there."

"Should I call your mom to let her know you have left and why?"

"I called her early this morning to let her know I would be in New York. She mentioned she would call you so you and Charlie could come over."

As he walked to the door, she patted his arm, "We will be thinking of you, Michael." It seemed so long ago he had been angry and upset. Michael was a different person who could show his weaknesses.

He slowly closed the door. Emma went to the front window to watch the taxi backing out. She turned to look at Charlie, sleeping soundly with her hand curled under her head.

At that moment, she felt alone. But, she was now encouraged by Michael's courage to deal with his issues. She would pick up a burner phone tomorrow, she promised herself. I wish I had thought about it before, she thought to herself. She planned to finish decorating the rest of the tree soon. But, for now, she would enjoy the solitude and the fragrance of the evergreen for a few minutes.

As the dusk came early that December afternoon, Emma hung the two new ornaments she had bought the day before. She stepped back to admire them. One was a quilt pattern ornament. The other was a weathervane, the closest decoration she could find that looked like a whirligig. She unfolded the Christmas quilt on the floor to admire it. It was beautiful. Charlie immediately crawled over to it and laid her head down. The colors were greens and reds, and the patterns were charming. She wondered how she won the quilt. Who would have put her name in enough times to win the quilt? She would quiz Michael when he returned.

Charlie was sitting up now and was playing with the toys Olivia had found for her. "Let's have dinner and hope Michael calls us soon. He should be there by now." He was somewhere in New York, although he hadn't mentioned the network offices.

Emma heated up leftover mac and cheese, which was easy and fun for Charlie. Emma wasn't hungry and thought she might eat later. Just as she was about to take Charlie upstairs to bed, she heard the phone ring.

"Hello?" she said, relieved as she heard Michael's voice. She shifted Charlie to her other side to hold the phone. He said the flight was okay, and he was waiting to talk to one of the cable executives. He hoped they were doing okay, and she assured him they were.

Michael had remembered that he hadn't bought a burner phone for her but would when he returned. Emma was okay with waiting as she had waited that long to contact her parents. At least she could call before Christmas Day.

Emma ended the call and hoped he would get the answers he wanted. They both sat on the Christmas quilt and played with her toys. Early that evening, she took Charlie upstairs and got her ready for bed. She had been rubbing her eyes, and Emma thought she was tired. After coming back downstairs, the night seemed endless before her, and she almost changed her mind to finish decorating the house when a key rattling in the front door startled her.

Who would be coming by when she had just talked to Olivia earlier that afternoon? And who else had a key?

She walked over as the door opened to see a tall, beautiful blond woman dressed in an elegant suit. With her hair in a fashionable know and gold jewelry sparkled in the porch light, she was sophisticated.

"May I help you?" Emma asked, confused.

"And who are you? Why are you here? Where is Michael?" All was said arrogantly with her chin up.

"I am his housekeeper. Who are you?"

"I am his fiancée!" she said as she pushed past Emma in the doorway, hitting her in the shin with her enormous suitcase.

Emma was speechless for a moment but closed the door to keep out the cold. She rubbed her hurt leg.

"Oh, the house looks pretty with the tree," the woman said as she set down her luggage. "What a perfect setting for a Christmas wedding!"

Emma was startled but managed to say, "I thought you and Michael had broken up before leaving on his last assignment."

"Just a little misunderstanding! I called the network yesterday, and they said he was back here in his hometown. I think he decided our marriage was more important than that simple job. It takes him worldwide, and he leaves for months at a time. So where is he anyway?"

"He is in New York, talking to network executives," Emma answered.

"Oh well, he will be home shortly, I think. I want dinner right after I take a hot shower. My trip here was exhausting. A nice steak would hit the spot," the woman said as she headed upstairs. "Oh, and bring up my suitcase; I will be in Michael's room."

Emma just stared at her backside, sashaying as she went upstairs. She didn't want to rock the boat with this woman, so she took the luggage up and placed it in the hall outside Michael's room. She could hear the shower running in the bathroom. Emma didn't know whether to laugh or cry.

Luckily, Charlie had fallen asleep and hadn't made a sound. The woman might freak out if she saw a baby in the house with the housekeeper. Emma went back to the kitchen to defrost a steak. After dinner, she would call Olivia to see what she thought about the woman barging abruptly. Emma baked potato, made a salad and opened a bottle of wine. It seemed silly to make the meal for just one, so she prepared it for them both. Charlie had been happy with macaroni and cheese, her favorite.

Emma set the table for two and worked on the rest of the meal. Finally, the woman came down in a silky robe with her hair flowing around her head. She looked as if she planned a night of seduction with her supposed fiancé, even if he wasn't home.

The uninvited guest stood at the kitchen door, looking at the table set for two. "Oh dear, I don't eat with hired help. It would be best if you ate somewhere else. Thanks for the wine selection, though. It is one of my favorites because Michael and I bought it while on vacation in Napa Valley. I am ready for dinner now."

Emma just stared at her and removed her place setting. "Serve yourself. I need to see Charlie."

"Who in the hell is Charlie?" she asked in an abrasive tone.

Emma was beyond being friendly to this shrew. "My child just woke up. I will stay upstairs while you eat, and I will eat after you finish. Just put your dishes in the dishwasher."

"How rude you are. A servant would never be that way. Michael needs to know you are behaving as if you own the place."

Emma nearly laughed aloud as the woman sounded like she lived in England in the 1800s. Right now is America in the twenty-first century. Emma chuckled as she walked up the stairs. She could keep Charlie occupied while the woman ate her steak and drank her wine. Maybe she would get drunk, which would serve her right!

Emma went to Charlie's room to pick up the crying child. A sound must have awakened her; maybe the slamming of Michael's door when the no-name lady came downstairs. Emma could not remember her name. Someone must have mentioned it.

As Charlie and Emma sat on the floor of her tiny bedroom, she listened for steps coming upstairs. Charlie was delighted to have Emma sitting on the floor and playing with her toys. She loved to crawl around, grabbing at her stuffed animals, especially. Emma believed children learn well when adults talk to them to understand every word. Her beginning studies to become a teacher had included an excellent course in child development. That class had helped in raising her niece, especially under the circumstances.

Finally, she heard the woman come upstairs and go into Michael's room. She could now go down to eat. Charlie had already eaten, but she took her downstairs so she wouldn't cry.

Emma was not surprised to see the plate and silverware still on the table. She had made no effort to take her dishes to the dishwasher. How could Michael have thought this woman was good enough to be a decent wife? Instead, she had taken her wine glass and bottle to Michael's room. Emma chuckled. Maybe the woman took it up to soothe her evil soul. Emma didn't suffer fools easily. Although she had another steak defrosted, she had lost her appetite and decided to heat Charlie's mac and cheese.

She carried Charlie into the living room for the sparkling Christmas tree lights. Emma realized there were tears in her eyes with thoughts swirling around her head. Maybe she had been living in dreamland with Michael. She felt so comfortable around him and admired him for his determination to deal with Afghanistan's events. They caused him nightmares, and it took courage to face the issue head-on. She hoped the network would be able to get him some help.

Charlie started to drift off. Emma turned off the Christmas tree lights, the front porch lights, and the kitchen lights. She left one night light on over the staircase if the lady came down. Emma laughed at the thought of the no-name woman. Someone must have mentioned her name, but Emma couldn't remember it. She thought of calling Olivia but had left the house phone downstairs. She would do it in the morning.

CHAPTER THIRTY-FIVE

...in which Emma gets the skinny on her obnoxious guest

The following day Emma was up early, hoping to hear back from Michael. She was eager to share the events of the previous day. The obnoxious guest had not come down by 11, so Emma decided to take Charlie out. They would go over to Olivia's house to see what she thought.

She bundled Charlie up because the temperatures were dropping. Emma hoped the weather wouldn't bring on another snowstorm so that Michael couldn't get back. The day would drag on if they didn't hear from him.

The walk to Olivia's house didn't take long, but she didn't come to her door. So Emma went around the block to Millie's house. Maybe they were having coffee together. But, again, no one answered the door. Disappointed but not ready to give up, she pushed the stroller farther down the street to Molly's Market. She thought picking up food for Christmas Eve would cheer her up.

"Hi, Emma," said Charlotte, the girl from the bakery department. "What are you two doing out today? It has gotten a little colder for sure. I always wish for snow for Christmas."

"Hi Charlotte, I haven't seen you since Thanksgiving. Are you okay?"

"Sure, just took a few days off here and there to keep up with holiday shopping. Molly is good with part-timers."

"I think I will pick up some food for Christmas Eve dinner. My family always had a buffet of sandwiches and salads before opening stocking stuffers. So I think I will do that for Michael."

"Michael's back?" Charlotte asked, with a puzzled look on her face. "I thought he was in Afghanistan. Olivia didn't mention it to me."

Emma replied quietly, "He came back early. I am not sure why, though."

"I am sure he appreciates someone taking care of him. His ex-fiancée was a horror. I am glad the witch broke it off last summer."

"What was she like?"

"Well, every time I had to deal with her, she was insulting, thinking that she was sophisticated and clever. So, I just thought she was selfish, and it puzzled me that Michael would want to marry her."

Emma decided not to mention that the rude lady had barged into the house just yesterday. "You never know a person's preference when it comes to love."

"Well, good luck with your shopping. I just saw Millie and Olivia chatting at the butcher counter. Guess Millie is buying her usual roast for Christmas dinner. They have been celebrating the holidays together ever since their husbands died. They enjoy sharing Christmas dinner with the boarding house residents."

"I know what you mean. Olivia and Millie have helped Charlie and me in the last month. I think I will go find them and ask what we can bring to Christmas dinner."

Charlotte laughed, "I doubt it would be Christmas without you, Charlie, and Michael now that he is home."

"Come on, Charlie, let's go find Olivia and Millie and see what they think."

As they went through the aisles, Charlie started reaching out for colorful boxes on the shelves. Emma just turned her stroller away slightly and showed her something else.

"Hi, ladies," she said as she headed to the counter where the butcher showed Olivia and Millie a big fresh roast.

"That's perfect. Could you wrap it up?" Millie asked, obviously pleased with her purchase. "Hello, girls, what are you up to today?"

"Hi, Olivia, hi Millie, so good to see you."

"What's wrong? You look stressed. Did Michael call you from New York?"

"He did, but something else happened that has shaken me."

"What happened?" As she picked up Charlie, who was starting to squirm in her stroller, Olivia asked.

"Michael's fiancée showed up last night and was so rude, and I still don't know her name."

"What is Allison doing back here? She left in a huff last summer and gave Michael back her engagement ring."

"Now I remember. Someone must have told me Allison's name. I just forgot. She thinks he has decided to give up his career and come back to the states permanently because he came home early. She has moved into his bedroom as if she owns it. I am not sure I should tell Michael that she is here, but I would hate him to be surprised."

"Has he called again? I called him last night after he spoke to you. He sounded hopeful even before he talked to the network executives."

"I know. Michael sounded optimistic."

"I think we owe you thanks for helping him."

"He was a great help when I got sick earlier this month. He took care of Charlie very well. I still laugh thinking about him carrying her around like a football."

Both women chuckled as they thought of the sight of Michael with a small child.

"Looks as if you have a great prime rib roast there. What else do you need for Christmas dinner? I hope Michael will get home before Christmas Eve."

"Michael has missed several holidays in the past few years. I think he will try to get back if he can," Olivia admitted.

"Do you all like spinach soufflé? I can make that. Not sure how Christmas will be with our uninvited guest, but what if I hosted on Boxing Day? My parents always hosted a brunch the day after Christmas. It was fun to see neighbors who might have sent their families home. It used to be a celebration for servants who worked in big homes."

"Great idea, Emma! "

"Let's plan as if Michael will be home, and Allison will be gone. I can't imagine Michael taking her back after her behavior last summer."

"Merry Christmas, ladies, " said the butcher as he put the large roast in their basket.

"Same to you," they all said in unison.

"Good luck," Millie said to Emma, winking, "Especially with Allison! She is a piece of work. We never knew what Michael saw in her."

As they left the store, a quiet group went back to their homes. They all thought about Michael's challenges, both in his mental health and with the woman waiting for him.

CHAPTER THIRTY-SIX

...in which soft-boiled eggs are the last straw

Emma opened the door and put the stroller in the hallway. She didn't pick up Charlie, who had fallen asleep. Instead, she carefully took her coat but left Charlie in the stroller.

"Where in the hell have you been?" yelled Allison from the hallway as Emma came into the living room. It was strange knowing her name finally. "I wanted my breakfast, and you were gone. What kind of housekeeper are you anyway?"

"I am Michael's housekeeper, not yours," she said, standing in front of Charlie. Emma didn't think she even noticed her in the stroller.

"Well, since we are getting married, get over it. Get to work. I want two soft-boiled eggs and toast. And of course, coffee." She huffed as she went back into Michael's bedroom and slammed the door.

Charlie looked puzzled but didn't cry over the outburst. Her behavior surprised Emma because calm people had always surrounded her. Emma again didn't know whether to laugh or cry. After changing her, she quietly walked up the stairs and put Charlie in her crib. Emma calmly talked to her to see if she would fall back asleep. "Well, I guess I could fix something. I wouldn't mind a piece of toast myself."

She headed downstairs and filled a pot to heat for the eggs. For the life of her, she couldn't think of anything mean to do to this witch. Mustard on the toast? Oh, it wasn't worth the trouble!

She set the eggs for four minutes. That's what her mom always did for her and her sister on cold winter mornings. She was daydreaming about her childhood and feeling melancholy all of a sudden. She also missed Michael, which was ironic, as he had scared her when they first met Thanksgiving evening.

Emma was about to call up the stairs that the breakfast was ready when Allison appeared in the doorway in wool slacks and a very expensive sweater. "Well, it's about time," she said as she sat down.

The woman put the napkin in her lap and turned to Emma, and said, "Better pack your bags, honey. As soon as Michael returns from his trip, he will fire you after I tell him how awful you were with me."

Emma had her back turned as she washed the pot from boiling the eggs. She almost laughed out loud but slowly turned around and asked, "Can I get you anything else?"

"No," Allison replied curtly.

Emma quietly walked out of the kitchen and into the living room, where she turned on the Christmas tree lights. She sat down in the oversized chair she thought was so comfortable. Emma pulled up her legs under her and thought about what might happen when Michael returned. He left for thirty-six hours, and she hadn't heard from him since the first call.

"Well, I am going out to see if there are any decent shops in this backwater town. I will eat lunch in town but will be back by dinner. There had better be something ready for my dinner," Allison said with her hands on her hips.

Emma looked at her but didn't reply. There was no reason to answer, as she had no intention of making any meals for her ever again. Allison slammed the front door. Emma breathed a little easier as she could hear her car leaving the driveway. How could anyone live with someone as nasty as Allison was beyond Emma?

It would serve Allison right if Emma and Charlie went to Olivia's house late afternoon and evening. She doubted Michael would be back that night. Emma put her head back and stretched out with her feet on the matching ottoman. She thought that Michael had great taste in comfortable furniture even though he traveled for many weeks with his job and was hardly ever home. It must be a difficult life, but he used his writing talents as a journalist.

She fell asleep and woke when she heard Charlie murmuring in her crib. Funny, she hardly ever woke up crying. Emma wondered if Charlie would remember her mother. She would show her photographs of her mother and talk about her often.

"Hi, Little Bits!" Emma said to Charlie, peeking around the corner of the door. Nothing like a baby to make one feel better. "What do you say? Let's call Olivia and ask her if we can come over? We might ask her if we could stay for the night. I am not sure I can stay here with the witch," Charlie smiled as if she understood.

They went downstairs to call Olivia, who said they could come over. Olivia understood how difficult Allison could be.

Emma packed an overnight bag but decided to leave a note for Allison, although she didn't deserve it. She wouldn't say where she was but that she was out for the night.

The walk over to Olivia's took little time. The weather was brisk, but the winds had died down. The snow had partly melted, and the sidewalk was clear, which helped push the stroller.

"Hello girls," Olivia said as she hugged Emma and picked up Charlie. Interestingly, Emma felt she had known Olivia for years. So even if Michael didn't come back the next day, she would go into town and buy a burner phone to call her mother and father.

"I found some building blocks in the attic that used to be Michael's. Do you think Charlie is old enough to play with them? They were hand-made by his dad when he was just a young boy."

"I think she might be old enough, but I might have to teach her not to throw them." They both laughed at the thought.

"Let's put down this blanket with the blocks on top while we make dinner. I hope you don't mind. I asked Millie to come over."

"Of course not. Millie is one of my favorite people ever."

Charlie picked up the blocks, but they showed her how to play with them. She also knocked them all over the floor and laughed. That kept her occupied for about fifteen minutes, and then she started crawling around. Emma just followed her around to prevent her from getting into Olivia's things.

"Oh, my goodness!" Millie hollered as she opened the back door to the kitchen. "What has the witch done now?"

Emma assumed she meant Allison but was not sure she knew her well. "What did Olivia tell you?"

"That she barged into Michael's home without a thought and was as obnoxious as ever. I was happy when she broke off their engagement last summer."

"You both knew her pretty well, I guess," Emma commented, shrugging her shoulders.

"The longer we knew her, the less we liked her. It always puzzled me that Michael asked her to marry him," Olivia said, picking up some of the blocks scattered all over the floor. "Michael always had an eye for blonds, although I doubt she is a real blond," she said, winking at Emma.

"Should we warn Michael that she is back?" Emma asked both women.

"Allison left with no doubts about her lack of support for his career. I understand that it is hard to have a loved one going to dangerous places," Olivia added.

"I think it would be more fun to watch the fireworks when he does come back," Millie said.

Emma thought to herself that he would have to be honest with her if the noise level of the fireworks would cause him issues.

"Allison has no idea why he came back and the issues he is facing. Michael could be going through a rough patch for some time while he works through them. Michael just shared the situation with me. I think he also shared it with you before he left for New York," Emma said, looking at Olivia.

His mother looked sad but hugged Emma. "Yes, he called before he left. I thought it involved the young man who traveled with him and videotaped his reports to send back to the network. He seemed to be angry about something that had happened. I didn't think it was wise to press the issue. He would have talked to his dad earlier he was still alive."

"We just visited Stanley's parents yesterday, and they were glad to see Michael. They have set up a scholarship at the Mizzou in Stanley's name. I think that comforted Michael. He made a whirligig in honor of Stanley and gave it to the Abernathys. I think just the effort and work of making it for them was therapeutic for Michael."

Charlie started pounding blocks on the floor. They all wandered to the kitchen where Millie had come through the door. Emma thought about how a child can bring difficult conversations back to the ordinary. Charlie pulled herself up on the kitchen chair and took a slight step over to the next chair. Emma kept her arms around her slightly to catch her if she fell. She probably would have lots of tumbles as she experimented.

Their attention then focused on preparing dinner. The ladies always made Emma feel better and more lighthearted. There was an improvement just being out of Michael's house and away from the tension.

The phone rang, and Olivia answered, hoping it would be Michael. However, she was unsure she would tell him of Allison's surprise arrival.

"Well, hello, Allison. Where are you these days?" Olivia looked over at Emma and Millie and winked. "Hadn't seen you since last summer when you broke off the engagement. I hope you are doing well, wherever you are," said Olivia, winking again at Millie and Emma.

"You are at Michael's? Whatever for?" she responded, smiling, listening to Allison's reply.

"She what? Oh my! I haven't seen Emma in ages. We have been busy with the Christmas pageant preparations at church and the town holiday festival. I can't imagine where she would be—maybe shopping."

It seemed Olivia was not above telling little white lies when the circumstances dictated it.

"I am sure you can find something to eat in the refrigerator or freezer. Emma has been cooking since Michael came back."

"No, no, I don't know when Michael will return home. He went to network headquarters a few days ago, I think."

"Take care, Allison." Olivia gladly ended the conversation. Hanging up the phone, she said, "Whew! She is the same old Allison, that's for sure. She was always arrogant and demanding. I was so relieved when she called off the engagement."

"Guess she was mad I wasn't there to cook her dinner."

"That she was for sure. I can't believe she still had keys to the house."

"Well," Millie said, "Let's forget her and make dinner. Would either of you be interested in playing Tripoly, my favorite card game?"

"Is it hard to learn?" Emma asked.

"Not at all. It is a combination of Poker and Michigan Rummy. Lots of fun."

"Michigan Rummy is fun, and I have played Poker before," said Emma.

Dinner around the kitchen table was fun as the women shared Michael's stories from his childhood. He was all boy and always involved in a sport or activity. He and his friends, including Millie's son, Atticus, had a fort in the woods behind their houses and spent hours there with all types of adventures.

"Oh my, my sister and I had a fort in the woods behind our house. So your son's name is Atticus? "Emma asked. "Isn't that the character who was a lawyer in To Kill a Mockingbird?"

"It is. My husband, Joe, loved the book and the play. Atticus is a lawyer in Atlanta, Georgia. Funny how life turns from fiction to real life."

The evening proved to be a great distraction to all three women. Even Charlie enjoyed all the lively conversation and camaraderie. The Tripoly game was new to Emma, but she caught on right away and enjoyed it, winning the jackpot several times.

Charlie started to yawn, so Olivia told her to go upstairs to the first guest room in the hallway. There was a big queen-sized bed they could both use.

"Thank you both for a great evening. I was rather depressed thinking about Michael and Allison. He could do better than a woman like her." Emma admitted.

"I think so!" they both said in unison, laughing.

"Good night, you two," Emma said.

"Good night, Sweet Pea," said Olivia giving both Charlie and Emma a peck on the cheek.

As Emma took the stairs, she realized these women had become part of her family and loved them. Michael came into her life like an angry hurricane and became a friend. Emma felt guilty that she had been too afraid to call her parents. Had she overreacted to the threats that Phillip had made about the baby? Did Emma leave town before thinking it through? Maybe the danger was not as bad as they thought. Guilt seemed to hover over her like a cloud, but she was determined to protect Charlie from Phillip.

She tucked Charlie into the big bed, low to the ground. Then she put a rolled-up blanket on both sides to keep the baby in the same spot. Charlie was a sound sleeper, so it should be fine. Emma fell asleep listening to the quiet conversation downstairs, feeling comforted.

chapter thirty-seven

*...in which Emma has doubts but
Allison gets her just desserts*

Sunday morning, Emma woke early and sat in the chair by the window, thinking about her family. She continued to have doubts about running away with Charlie and not communicating with her parents for so many weeks. The two phone calls with four rings were pretty lame, but it is what they had agreed to quickly the night Emma left. She missed Michael. She hoped his visit with the network executives went well and that he also had an appointment with the therapist in St. Louis on his way home.

The day went by quickly as the four of them went to church in the morning. They then had brunch at The Chicken Café before going back to the church to help with the Christmas pageant's final rehearsal, which would be Christmas Eve. Emma volunteered to help with costumes. She took over the duty of fixing the sheep costumes. Unfortunately, some of the little bells had fallen off. However, it was easy to sew them back on. Charlie enjoyed being in the playpen in the workroom as all the children came over to talk to her. It had been a long time since the town had a young child.

They returned to Olivia's and decided to make a simple soup and then get a good night's sleep before Christmas Eve the next day.

The morning of Christmas Eve dawned a little foggy, but with a hint of snow in the air. As Emma looked out the window of Olivia's guest room, she hoped that Michael could make it back for a holiday. She wished he would have called the night before, but she understood he might be home soon.

Charlie had already been wide-awake before Emma opened her eyes. The baby touched her on her cheeks and then fell against her as they hugged. Laying in a cozy bed with a child on a winter day felt like heaven on earth. She stayed still and just smelled Charlie's baby smell. On closer reflection, she needed a change of diaper for sure.

They both dressed in warm clothes. Charlie wore a reindeer sweater Emma had found at a store downtown. They headed down the stairs when Emma could smell the coffee and frying bacon. She almost expected Millie to be still sitting there as she left them last night, but only Olivia stood at the stove with the bacon sizzling.

"Is there any better smell in the morning?" Emma asked, putting Charlie in the highchair on loan from Millie's attic. Charlie immediately started pounding the tray and laughing.

"Have you heard from Michael?" asked Emma.

"He did call and told me that he would try to be back this afternoon. He said he would text us when he arrived. He mentioned that the phone at his home rang and rang, but no one picked it up. Michael was glad you had come over to stay with us last night. I am afraid I did not tell him of the surprise visitor, though. I can't tell you how he will react, but I don't think he will welcome her with open arms. She left their relationship very badly, and he was upset at first."

"I can't believe you didn't tell him Allison is here expecting their relationship to be the same," Emma said, chuckling. "That will be quite the scene, I think."

After eating breakfast, they sat at the kitchen table and talked about what could happen. Emma felt that maybe Olivia knew something she wasn't telling her, but she didn't mention it. "I almost wish I could be a fly on the wall to see the scene when Michael sees Allison in his home."

"Well, maybe we could if Michael sends us a text on his way to the house. I think he was going to grab a taxi from the train station. We could run over and pretend we know nothing." They both started giggling like two little girls. Charlie joined in with the laughter.

"Why don't you help me prepare part of Christmas dinner while we wait to hear from him? You could help organize the makings for the Yorkshire pudding. We can put it together tomorrow while the roast is roasting. Michael loves mashed potatoes, so we can make a potato casserole ahead of time. Would you mind peeling the potatoes? Less to do tomorrow."

"Yes to all of it. Reminds me of being home," Emma said, a little sadly. "But I am happy to have found you all."

"Especially, Michael?" asked Olivia with a bit of twinkle in her eye.

"Oh, I don't know. Michael was kind while I was sick during the snowstorm and was great with Charlie, although a little unorthodox in his methods," she said, remembering how he carried her around like a football.

The morning and early afternoon quickly passed after Millie came over with sandwiches for lunch and the ingredients for a salad for Christmas dinner. Charlie took a little nap and then had a small snack when the phone rang. Olivia answered and said, "Thanks for calling, Michael. We will come over to meet you."

They all hurried with coats and scarves and made their way around the corner to Michael's house. They decided to go in before Michael got there to see his reaction to Allison. They noticed her car in the driveway.

Emma used her key and stepped inside, letting the ladies enter first into the living room. The Christmas lights were off, and the room was dark. They all looked at each other, wondering where Allison was.

"Michael, about time. I have been waiting for you for two days!" She shouted from the upstairs hallway.

Olivia spoke up first, saying, "Sorry, Allison, just us. We came over for Christmas Eve dinner here. Is Michael not here?"

"No, and I haven't heard from him," she said. "Who invited you to dinner?"

"Emma planned it for all of us!" Olivia said, patting Emma on her shoulder.

"The housekeeper?" Alison asked with a scornful snort. "She hasn't taken good care of me."

"You were uninvited, you know. "

"Michael won't mind that I came."

"I thought you had called off the engagement last summer. Have you reconciled?"

"Well, he has come home. That tells me he will not be traveling anymore. I think that is a positive sign for me. I think it would be wise if Emma were gone before he returns. It will not be a pretty picture when I tell him how she treated me. Why did he need a housekeeper when he wasn't even in the country?" Alison asked.

"I hired her because I couldn't take care of my house and his house. It was too much for me," Olivia admitted.

Allison made a grunt and headed for the kitchen. "I need a drink!" she said, talking to no one in particular.

Emma heard a car pull into the driveway. She held her breath as she waited for Michael to come through the door.

"Hello, everyone. Hello, Little Bits," Michael said, heading straight for Charlie, who had her arms open wide for him" She touched his nose as he held her. Then, looking over at Emma, he said, "Missed you both! And Mom and Millie, of course," he added, looking at them also. "Why do you still have your coats? What's going on?"

"I guess a little surprise," Olivia said.

Just at that moment, Alison came around the corner from the kitchen, holding a bottle of red wine and a glass. "Hello, Michael, about time you got home!"

"What are you doing here, and why are you drinking my wine?"

"I heard you had returned to the states, and I just knew you wanted to resume our engagement."

"I returned because something happened with my crew, and I needed to help recover myself."

"You were hurt?" she asked, sincerely concerned.

"Not physically, but it is a long story. Allison. I don't mean to be rude, but our engagement is over. It would be best if you left right now. My returning has nothing to do with you."

Allison just stared at him and said, "Well, it looks like rudeness surrounds me today. Your housekeeper was terrible to me and barely fixed my meals. I told her you would fire her when you got back."

Michael laughed and said, "Hardly, I would have told her not to fix you anything if I had known. He handed Charlie back to Olivia and said, "Here, let me take the bottle and glass so you can go upstairs and pack. We will wait while you do."

Allison turned with a red face, her hands curled into fists, but her chin turned up with her straight back. She walked up the stairs as Michael turned and looked at Emma with an apologetic look.

"So sorry, Emma, that Allison treated you so rudely. I can't believe I forgot to get the house key back from her last summer."

"It wasn't too bad, but I had never dealt with such a self-serving person before. She was sure your return to the states was a message to her that you wanted her back. What kind of person would think that?" Emma looked at them all with a shrug of her shoulders.

They all turned as Allison came downstairs with her suitcase banging down the steps. She looked furious, and her hair was all over her face. She stopped at the bottom and looked over at Michael, who held Charlie, who kept touching his nose affectionately.

"Well, whose baby is that? Were you unfaithful to me, Michael? I could believe that, I think."

"No, this is my housekeeper's child, although it is none of your business. Please leave now. We are getting ready for Christmas Eve dinner. Don't forget the door key. Just put it on the table."

Allison must have decided the game was over. She turned, went out the door, and slammed it behind her.

Olivia and Millie started laughing, and Olivia said, "I wouldn't have missed that for anything. I never liked her, but this was even a worse side of her than I ever saw before."

Michael looked relieved, but he also seemed exhausted to Emma, "Why don't you go up to take a shower, and we will get food out for dinner. Do you all attend Christmas Eve services?" She knew Michael would have more issues to deal with before he would be okay. She hoped he might share what happened in New York with her later.

"Yes, we do. The church has several services!" Olivia answered. "Would Little Bits be able to sleep through one of them?"

"What about an earlier time? It might be better than a later service. She might fall asleep during a later service."

"I know they have the Christmas pageant at the earlier service, so Charlie might enjoy seeing the kids act out the nativity scene. The pageants have been fun, always heartwarming and sometimes funny," said Millie.

Michael headed to the stairs but turned and shared his memory, "Remember the year someone brought a goat for the manger scene, and he started chewing on the kids' costumes. I remember the children and the audience laughing so hard that they couldn't finish for a few minutes."

Emma laughed and watched as Michael continued up the stairs.

"How do you think he is?" Olivia asked as she put her arm around Emma's shoulder.

"Not sure. Michael was surprised by Allison's appearance. I guess he will share more later," Emma replied as they headed to the kitchen.

CHAPTER THIRTY-EIGHT

...in which Charlie meets a Baby Jesus

Christmas Eve

After Emma put out the meal, she thought back to her parents' holiday dinners with dollar rolls, ham, Swiss cheese, deviled eggs, and potato salad. It was casual but always delicious. She called to Michael that dinner was ready.

He came down in a warm sweater and corduroy slacks. His hair was still wet and combed back from his face. Emma thought he was more relaxed than he had been. He smiled at them all as he sat down. No one said anything until Millie said, "Let's say a little prayer of grace."

They all held hands, even Charlie, who had hold of Michael and Olivia's hands, and closed their eyes. "Thank you for our health, for being together on this Christmas Eve, and we pray for those who are not with us tonight."

"Amen!" they all said in unison. Charlie just laughed and banged the highchair tray with a small spoon Olivia had given her. Michael thought he saw a little wistfulness in Emma's eyes, but she blinked and said, "Let's pass the food. There is plenty."

Michael was sure that she missed her mom, dad, and especially her sister. He sighed but winked at Olivia, who immediately looked away.

The meal had always been a buffet with Emma's family to admire their Christmas tree in the living room. She thought sitting at the kitchen table was the right thing to do this night. Emma felt loved by her adopted family, but she missed her mother and father. With all the turmoil Allison had brought with her, Emma forgot about buying a burner phone, which she should have done weeks ago. Maybe a store would be open on Christmas Day.

They all agreed to go to the Christmas Eve pageant, held around 7, so Charlie could have something fun to watch and maybe wouldn't fall asleep.

As they left Michael's home around 6:30, they were delighted to see flakes of snow drifting to the ground. The streets were just wet, but the snow was sticking to the grass.

"How beautiful!" Emma said.

Charlie stuck her tongue out and tried to catch a snowflake on her tongue. "We tried that last time it snowed here, and she must have remembered," said Emma, wrapping a scarf more tightly around Charlie's neck. Emma nuzzled her neck and made her chuckle. "Could you be a happier baby?" she asked no one in particular as they made their way to the car. Michael lived just a short way from the church, so they made the trip in no time. The snow was not causing any trouble driving.

Olivia, Millie, Emma, Michael, and Charlie scooted to the middle of the pews. The three of them, who had lived in Hill Brook for a long time, knew people for years. Nice to have a church family, Emma thought as she looked through the crowd. Michael sat next to his mother, and Emma sat down next to him. She knew the girl from Molly's, Charlotte, and Joe Hampton, who was sitting next to Elizabeth, smiling happily. Emma smiled back and wondered if that was something new for Joe. There were many smiling faces she had met in Hill Brook in just a couple of months. She was glad to see them all. When Emma saw Josh and Amy walk in together, Emma smiled.

She turned around to see Ella Rose and her grandparents in the next pew. Charlie couldn't keep her eyes off the chandeliers that were glowing in the evening darkness. Emma unwrapped her from her little snowsuit. Michael took it and put it on the space on the aisle. Charlie discovered standing on the pew and looked at the people on the bench behind her. She was grinning at everyone. Emma hoped the service wouldn't be too long. She was sitting next to Michael and could feel him moving around, keeping Charlie from falling. Considering how angry he had been on Thanksgiving, he couldn't have been kinder to both of them since then.

The music began about that time, and the organ pipes startled Charlie. Michael turned her around so she could see the pageant beginning. The minister started with a blessing. Then, the choir sang "O' Come All Ye Faithful." Next, the children came to the front of the sanctuary and started telling the story of Jesus' birth. Emma thought they performed well and had clear voices with the microphones. Charlie seemed mesmerized by the action. Suddenly, three children dressed as shepherds came down the aisle with their crooks. Next came the children dressed as all kinds of animals. Charlie clapped her hands, especially when she saw the sheep with bells on their necks. Emma thought they looked cute, and she remembered repairing all the bells the previous week.

The procession to the altar continued with Joseph, Mary, and the shepherds. The kings came next. She looked at the group at the altar and noticed that Mary and Joseph were sitting around a wooden manger. There was a baby waving arms and legs, obviously a newborn. It was always special when the congregation had a family with a baby to play Jesus rather than a doll.

Finally, the angels came next in beautiful white costumes with sparkling halos. The halos were slipping over eyes. They all held decorated staffs with more bells. Emma had tears in her eyes from the scene as they gathered around the manger.

The best was yet to come. Everyone had received a small unlit candle on entering the sanctuary. Ushers went about lighting all the candles. The entire church was dark, and with just the lights from the candles, everyone sang "Silent Night'. They sang the first verse in German, as the church heritage began with German immigrants in the 1830s. Olivia had told Emma about the tradition before they left for services. It was a beautiful sight. Everyone wished them a Merry Christmas. An usher had given Charlie a little battery candle to hold, and she was waving it around and chuckling. Emma felt better than she had in a long time. All she could have wished for was to have called home before now. Unfortunately, stores were closed by this time on Christmas Eve.

The lights came back on as the congregation was filing out. Of course, everyone around them made a fuss over Charlie. She started to cry when the usher tried to take the candle away. He thought better of it and let her keep it. She hugged it to her chest and smiled at the great gift.

The young teen who plays Mary came by them with the baby playing Jesus in her arms. Charlie looked over at her and wanted to pat the baby's cheek. Everyone around laughed at the sweet moment—several teenagers came to the writing club and said hi to Charlie, who loved the attention. Emma marveled at the simplicity of making her happy, at least at this age. Her teenage years may not be as easy as her toddler years. Emma just prayed she would be part of her life.

Michael held Charlie as Emma put her snowsuit back on when they came to the church's front door. They were shocked to see the snow had become heavier than it had been an hour before. It rarely snowed on Christmas Eve, but it was such a joy when it did. Emma heard the church Carillion playing Christmas carols as they walked to the car. It wasn't a clear night, but there were a few breaks in the clouds, and Emma could see stars peeking out. She thought it couldn't be a lovelier Christmas Eve, even if she missed her parents.

Heading back to Michael's home, the drive was a little trickier than the ride to church. Michael had a steady hand, and his four-wheel-drive car was strong enough to get through. Street crews had not had time to clear the streets and probably wouldn't until morning. Emma, Charlie, and Michael would walk over to Millie's home for Christmas dinner, even if the sidewalks had snow.

Olivia and Millie asked to be dropped off at Millie's house to prepare the Christmas feast for tomorrow. Michael got out to clear the sidewalk before they got out. Charlie started to cry when Michael left the car. She watched him as he retrieved the snow shovel from Olivia's porch and quickly cleared a path to the front door.

Emma thought about how Charlie had gotten attached to Michael in recent days. What would happen if he left for treatment somewhere? Maybe Michael would share with her what happened in New York. She wasn't sure if he had talked to his mom on the telephone about it. Olivia hadn't said anything to Emma.

The ride home was short, and Michael pulled the car into the garage. Neither one of them said anything until Michael said, "I will turn on the Christmas lights and make a small fire in the fireplace. I haven't been home for Christmas in a few years. I want this one to be special."

Emma took Charlie upstairs to put on her pajamas but brought her back down to enjoy the tree and the fire. Charlie probably would not remember this Christmas, but Emma had a few toys and things to open on Christmas Day, which she had tucked away behind the Christmas tree.

Michael opened a bottle of white wine, and Emma prepared a bottle for Charlie. They sat on the sofa and enjoyed the glow of the tree lights and the fire's flickering flames. It was peaceful, but Emma waited for Michael to say anything. Patience is a hard virtue, but she practiced it since Phillip had threatened to take Charlie away. His girlfriend didn't seem that interested in taking care of a baby, but they had hired a lawyer to push for custody for some reason. Emma was sure she was in trouble with the law for taking Charlie out of state without the father's approval. She had thought first that her parents should not know where she was if they had to testify. Maybe the court would take his horrible behavior during her sister's cancer treatment and death into account.

"You are quiet tonight," Michael said to Emma over Charlie's head.

"I guess I was waiting to see if you would share what happened while you were in New York."

"The network's HR Department recommended the therapist I saw in St. Louis, and they think he is perfect. I spoke with him again on the phone briefly, and we made several more appointments after the New Year."

"I think a therapist will be beneficial for you. Tomorrow I will call my parents, and maybe I can return home and let you recover in peace."

"I don't know. In my files, I have an iron-clad contract for a year's work," Michael said, grinning. "You would be breaking it if you left." He gave her a little hug.

Michael looked over at Charlie, sleeping in Emma's arms, and touched Emma's cheek. "I think I might recover better if you were here."

"Oh, Michael, do you mean it?"

He leaned over and gave her a kiss that showed promise.

She tucked Charlie onto her other arm, rested against Michael's shoulder, and felt perfect peace. She sighed but said nothing. They sat there for a long time, and finally, Emma said, "I better put Charlie to bed and get some sleep myself."

Michael kissed her again and kissed Charlie's cheek. "Just you two being here has made all the difference. I think I am better than I was."

Emma made her way upstairs, and Michael stayed downstairs for a little while. He knew his surprise would come tomorrow. It could make it a perfect Christmas Day.

CHAPTER THIRTY-NINE

...in which Christmas brings more than one surprise

Christmas morning dawned with crystal blue skies as it often does after a storm. Emma looked outside through the bedroom window, and she noticed that the snow cover was beautiful but not too deep. It was sparkling, like a million diamonds. Emma quickly dressed before Charlie woke up. She wore her warm sweater with the Christmas scene knitted into it, which she treasured for many years. Emma had grabbed it at the last minute while she was packing for the trip.

Although Charlie had not stirred, Emma decided to go downstairs to start the coffee. It would be nice to have a quiet breakfast before Charlie opened her gifts from Santa. It would be the first real Christmas since she was born the September before. She had been only four months old then. Since her mother had just died, the family did not feel like celebrating much of anything that year. However, this Christmas would be fun. Emma had bought her a few things, including a new doll.

As she got closer to the kitchen, she could hear noises in the pantry. Michael must be up and getting breakfast things. He came back carrying his cell phone, looking sheepish. "Did your mom just call about dinner tonight?" she asked.

Although he paused a few seconds before answering, he said, "Sure, she was just checking on what we are bringing for dinner."

Michael leaned back on the counter and pulled her into an embrace, and Emma fell into his arms. She rested her head on his chest and took a deep breath. He smelled like fresh soap. She looked up at him, and he kissed her gently. She felt so comfortable around him. She admired him for how he treated his mother and around Charlie. He was a big man but had a kind, gentle manner. Who could resist that?

"What do you say about Christmas breakfast with just us before we open presents?"

"You didn't have to buy gifts for us."

"I wanted to," he said, giving her a big hug and a kiss on her cheek. "What should we make for breakfast? How about waffles? I kept one engagement gift, a great waffle maker they use in restaurants. It works great, and it flips. It's the only gift I kept. It was from John, who insisted I keep it after Allison left in a huff."

Emma laughed. She thought he deserved it, and she had just dealt with Allison for just a brief time. Together they got the makings out, and Emma set the table in the kitchen. She thought about what future Christmases would bring? Where would she be, where would Charlie be? Maybe it would be best not to think about it.

Just about then, they both heard Charlie jumping and pulling on the crib. "Let me go up to get her while you mix up the batter," offered Michael.

"Her play clothes for this morning are on the dresser. I thought I would wait to put on her holiday outfit until we went to Millie's."

Emma could hear them talking from the bedroom while she made the waffles.

Michael was laughing and talking while he changed her diaper. Emma enjoyed listening to them chatter while he dressed her. Finally, they came down as Emma put bacon in the large black cast iron skillet. As Michael and Charlie came into the kitchen, Charlie said, "Mama." That startled

Emma, and tears streamed down her cheeks. It was a moment that neither Emma nor Michael would ever forget.

It seemed that Charlie felt the excitement for Christmas morning, even at her age. She was young enough not to mind sitting in the high chair as long as someone gave her some Cheerios to eat.

They made waffles with pecans, a plain one for Charlie, and maple-flavored bacon. The smell was delicious, and between them, they ate several waffles. Charlie loved to put cut-up pieces of waffles on her spoon and shove it in her mouth. She was beginning to control utensils, but she had more syrup on her fingers and mouth than inside her. Luckily Emma had bought her a Christmas bib in a store in town.

They cleaned up together and went into the living room. The tree sparkled gleaming with its colored lights. Around the tree were wrapped gifts that were not there the night before. Emma's presents for Charlie were behind the tree.

Charlie clapped her hands, and Emma sat her on the blanket on the floor. "Do we have time for a fire before we go to Millie's for dinner?"

"Of course, it wouldn't be Christmas without a cheery fire."

They settled in on the floor and handed Charlie different gifts, which she unwrapped with enthusiasm. She threw wrapping paper all over the floor. She loved the doll that Emma gave her. She held it in her arms just like she had seen others do. Next, Michael bought her a little racecar track set on an elevated spiral course. He and Emma set two cars at the top and guessed which one would first get to the bottom. Charlie clapped and bounced up and down. They had to do it over and over. Next, Michael handed Emma a little box wrapped in festive shiny paper with a beautiful bow. She hated to open it but was curious. Emma opened it without tearing the paper. She was so much in love with him she would save the wrapping forever and remember this moment. It was a beautiful gold necklace with a peace symbol in gold. "I picked it out because you had brought me peace when I thought I would never have it again."

"Michael, I love it. I will wear it always."

"Here is my gift for you. I hope you like it."

He opened the package and ripped the paper just like Charlie had. He was surprised to see a green scarf made out of Cashmere. It was beautiful.

"Thank you very much. Did you make it?"

"I did. When I was up later than Charlie, I would work on it before she woke up. I thought about you with every stitch."

They both leaned over and kissed while Charlie looked at them and clapped her hands.

They heard the front doorbell just as their kiss was ending. "Would you get that, Emma? I will clean up the wrapping paper."

"Sure! Would you keep an eye on Charlie?"

Emma went to the front door, expecting it might be Olivia or Millie, checking on something for dinner they had forgotten.

She opened the door and was shocked to see her parents on the doorstep.

"Oh, my goodness! Mom! Dad!" Emma shouted, reaching to hug them both. She then started to sob uncontrollably. Michael came up behind her with Charlie in his arms and put a hand on her shoulder. He was grinning from ear to ear as Emma turned to look at him.

"You did this, you, wonderful man!"

"Well, no doubt, I am, and I did, but let's have your parents come inside out of the cold."

"Of course, of course," she said, wiping tears from her face.

"I cannot believe how big Charlotte has gotten," Emma's mother said as she looked at her granddaughter. She wisely did not reach for her, as she wasn't sure that Charlie would recognize her. But within a few seconds, Charlie smiled broadly and wanted to be held. Michael handed her over to Emma's mother with a smile.

Her father closed the door and gave Emma another hug. They stayed that way for a few minutes. "I was terrified for you the night I dropped you off at the bus station in Salem. It was so dark, and the snow had started." Emma was afraid to ask what was happening with the lawsuit, so she said nothing. "I am so happy to see you."

Michael gave them space by walking into the kitchen, saying he would get them all some coffee.

They all sat down on the couch with Charlie looking back and forth between her mother and Emma. Finally, she reached up and touched Emma's dad on the nose, and he choked back tears.

"I am afraid to ask you what happened to Phillip and his girlfriend."

Her dad held her hand and said, "Well, at first, he was hysterical that you had taken Charlie and disappeared. We were glad we didn't know where you were so that we couldn't slip. We were also glad you rang the phone four times a few days after leaving. You did tell us you would do that when you ended up somewhere safe."

"I called from the train station when we arrived at Hill Brook. The name just sounded wonderful and safe for some reason. I was right. My friend, John, called you from Kansas City a week ago." She smiled when Michael came back into the room with mugs of coffee.

"Mr. and Mrs. Ingram, there is cream and sugar on the coffee table."

"Please, call us Harry and Madge. We are so grateful that you contacted us. You know, Emma, Michael stopped by on the way back from New York to talk to us. We were thrilled to know where you were and that you both were okay."

"It was no problem to visit them from New York. The train system was easy because Emma had given me your names and your city. My network was able to track down your address."

Emma was desperate to know what had happened with the custody lawsuit, so she exclaimed, "Well, what happened? Was the judge mad that I had taken Charlie out of state?"

"He never knew."

"What? How did that happen?"

"Well, Phillip was furious about it, but I feel he also felt a little guilty about how he treated Susie. His girlfriend is a little young and did not want to raise a child, let alone one who wasn't hers. So he never officially filed the lawsuit, although he implied that he had," Madge said.

"I was terrified when he showed up that one day with a gun in his coat pocket. He looked crazed. I recently started thinking maybe he was feeling a little guilty, although I doubt he would have said it. I think that's why I decided to leave. Thank you for your support, but maybe it would have been okay if I had stuck around. I have wondered about my motives for weeks. Was I selfish or just plain angry? Was I afraid we would lose Charlie? I have second-guessed myself recently."

"Don't be so hard on yourself, Sweetie. We have done the same thing."

"I came here for some reason," she said as she looked at Michael and smiled. "Michael suggested that I should have gotten a burner phone this week, and we could have been talking all this time. I am sorry I didn't think of it sooner."

"We heard through some friends that Phillip had figured out you had left town. Someone at the bus station told him you had a St. Louis ticket. So he hired some two-bit detective to look into it. Not sure how he found you were in Hill Brook."

"It was scary seeing a car drive by slowly and also hearing about the man who went to the B and B to ask questions," admitted Emma.

"It was just ten days ago that he withdrew his threat and decided to move away. Luckily, most people in our town had heard what he had done during Susie's illness, and no one supported him," her father added. "He left a message on our answering machine that he would sign a paper giving you complete custody," Harry said.

Emma felt a relief she had never felt before but didn't cry. She was so happy. She reached over to touch Charlie's cheek.

Emma finally realized her parents were probably starving. "How did you ever get a flight out of Newark Airport on Christmas Eve or Day? When did you leave?"

"Michael got the tickets, I suspect, with the company's travel department? He was so accommodating, making all the arrangements, including the car rental at the airport." Michael was busy adding a log to the fire and appeared not to be listening.

"This is the best Christmas ever," Emma said as she turned and hugged her parents as best she could with a baby in between.

"Michael, do you think Millie and your mom would mind two more guests coming tonight for Christmas Dinner?"

"Not at all. They are expecting your parents."

"You mean, they both knew about my parents coming?"

"I told Mom on the phone what we had arranged after I talked to Harry and Madge. I trusted her not to give the secret away. We wanted you to be surprised."

Michael came over and picked up Charlie, who had fallen asleep on her grandmother's shoulder. "I will put her down for a nap, and maybe you all would like to freshen up. The second room on the left is ready for you."

"I didn't even notice you had done that, Michael."

"I did it after you and Charlie had gone to sleep last night."

Michael took Charlie upstairs, and Harry followed Michael with their luggage.

Madge and Emma sat on the couch and just looked at each other. They had missed each other for the previous six weeks, especially when they felt they couldn't even talk on the phone.

"What are you going to do now, Emma? Are you thinking of coming home or staying here?"

"Not sure, but Michael is finally getting the help he needs for his PTSD. I think I might stay around to help him through the recovery."

"Has he shared the events with you?" her mom inquired.

"Yes, but it isn't my story to tell."

"I understand."

They sat quietly on the couch with hands clasped.

Madge finally said, "I think I will go up and wash my face. I did bring a change of clothes. We packed pretty fast. The airport this morning wasn't too crowded, and the car rental was fairly easy. Michael thought of everything, including needing a rental car. I was so excited; I couldn't put two thoughts together. He came to the house and introduced himself, as your employer and that you were his housekeeper. We laughed when we heard that. The story behind that must be unbelievable. You can tell us all about it this afternoon. I am very impressed with Michael. Although I don't know what happened to him, he seems to be dealing with it the right way."

"I have a lot to tell you. But, first, the people in Hill Brook have been wonderful. Millie and Olivia, I think, are my guardian angels. I can't wait for you to meet them later today. They somehow trusted me for a job and a place to live within just hours of knowing me."

Her mother hugged her and said, "I think you must have inspired them to trust you. I think I need to wash my face. As you know, I am not a morning person, and we had to be at the airport a little after dawn."

Emma laughed and watched as her mother walked up the stairs. It was so good to see them. What a great surprise and the news they brought was just what she had hoped would happen.

Michael came down the stairs and smiled broadly at Emma. Then, he came right over to the couch and put his arm around her. "Well, are you relieved?"

"You will never know how much all of it means to me."

"I think I know! What are you going to do now, Emma?"

"Mom said I could come back with them."

"What do you want to do?"

"Well, you probably do not need a housekeeper anymore."

"Oh no, remember that you cannot back out of an iron-clad contract," he said with a grin.

"You will hold me to that fake but well-intended contract?" she asked, remembering that John, Olivia, and Millie had devised it after Michael's return.

"I think you must take care of me in my time of need. Therapy could be very hard on me, and I need support from you and Charlie. I want you both to stay and be with me. You have become so important to me. I love having you around."

"You love having us around?"

"I love you, Emma. Is that clear enough? You have brought so much to me, my mom, in fact, anyone you meet. I love that you are a natural matchmaker. You even help teenagers have fun. Christmas has been so special with you."

"I love you, too, Michael. I will stand by you, no matter where your career goes or how therapy develops. I am so glad we visited Stanley's parents. I think that helped."

"The network is willing to let me out of my contact. I would like to do freelance writing about national news. I can do that anywhere. You mentioned you would like to go back to school. I remember you wanted to be a teacher. There is a great community college in Union with an easy commute."

"That would be perfect! I love to work with children, and taking care of Charlie has proved it to me."

Michael put his arm around her and pulled her onto his lap. "Let's seal the deal with a kiss?"

The kiss had great promise. When Emma's parents came back down the stairs, they grinned at each other and knew that things would work out for everyone. Today would be a wonderful Christmas, and Michael, Emma, and Charlie would be a unique family.

The Community Church Carillon around the corner started ringing a beautiful rendition of Christmas songs, heard all around Hill Brook. It made everyone in that house feel very special.

Emma leaned over and whispered in Michael's ear, "I'll stay if someone will tell me if there is a brook in Hill Brook." Michael laughed and kissed her again.